DEATH
OF A
ONE-SIDED MAN

DEATH
OF A
ONE-SIDED
MAN

The Frank May Chronicles

Lawrence Friedman

A QP Mystery

QP BOOKS
New Orleans, Louisiana

DEATH OF A ONE-SIDED MAN

The Frank May Chronicles

A QP Mystery, published in 2013 by QP Books.

QUID PRO, LLC
5860 Citrus Blvd., Suite D-101
New Orleans, Louisiana 70123
www.qpbooks.com

ISBN 978-1-61027-193-6 (pbk.)
ISBN 978-1-61027-189-9 (eBook)

Publisher's Cataloging-in-Publication

Friedman, Lawrence.
  Death of a one-sided man / Lawrence Friedman.
      p. cm.
    Series: *The Frank May Chronicles* (#6)
    ISBN: 978-1-61027-193-6 (pbk.)
1. Lawyers—California—Fiction. 2. San Mateo (Cal.)—Fiction. 3. May, Frank (Fictitious character)—Fiction. I. Friedman, Lawrence. II. Title. III. Series.
PS357.F779 2013   814.'7'3298—dc22
                                                              20134154737
                                                                      CIP

for Leah, Jane, Amy, Sarah,
David, Lucy, and Irene

Family Tree

Marylee Mobius (nee Hayden), wife of Piers Mobius, mother of Derek and Doris

Derek Mobius, son of Piers Mobius, grandson of Simon Mobius

Simon Mobius ("Grampa"; died at 82), widower

Piers Mobius (died in Australia), son to Simon, father to Derek, and ex-husband to Marylee

Doris Mobius, sister to Derek

Rupert Mobius (murdered, age 84), brother to Simon

Katerina Mobius and Cranshaw Mobius, children to Rupert

DEATH
OF A
ONE-SIDED MAN

1

When I read about the murder of Rupert Mobius in the *San Francisco Chronicle*, I had naturally no idea that I would soon find myself involved in this tawdry affair. I had never met Rupert Mobius, never heard of him in fact. The only reason I paid any attention at all to the story was that the name intrigued me. I'm a lawyer, and I once handled the estate of a woman named Cassandra Hayden. Ms. Hayden, an obnoxious elderly woman, left a small amount of money to a niece named Marylee Mobius. The name stuck in my mind. You meet lots of Smiths in California, and even more people named Garcia, Gomez, Wong, and Kim, but this was the first time I had come across a Mobius.

I guess that's why I noticed the short item in the *Chronicle*. Odd that somebody had murdered a Mobius. I wondered if this man could be connected to Marylee Mobius. After all, a Smith or a Chang or a Kim could meet an untimely death, and while this could no doubt be big news in some circles, the world would hardly notice one less Smith or Chang or Kim; but if you kill a Mobius, I said to myself, you might be seriously depleting the world's supply of Mobiuses. In fact, it might not take much to make the whole Mobius clan extinct, at least in the United States.

Extinction happened to be on my mind. I had just gotten the bad news about the Chinese river dolphin. This creature had been declared extinct. I found this sad. Not that I had been aware, to tell the truth, that there even *was* a Chinese river dolphin. At any rate, the dolphin had and has no connection at all to the death of Rupert Mobius. But, as you know, the mind is a funny thing. It jumps around like a drunken flea.

I never read any follow-up stories about Rupert Mobius and his mysterious death. For all I knew, the case had been solved. Or not. If I had to guess, I would have guessed that the whole thing was over and done with. The police had solved the case. They had surely arrested somebody and charged him with the crime. This is what usually happens.

The plain truth is, I was no longer reading the *San Francisco Chronicle*. In fact, I don't normally read the *Chronicle*. I live in San Mateo, which is not San Francisco at all, but a suburb to the south, down the peninsula. But one day a telemarketer called from the *Chronicle*, and offered me a month's subscription, "totally free. You can cancel at any time." I went for the bait. Celia—that's my wife—said I was being ridiculous. "They want you to buy a subscription at the end of the month, and we're not going to do it. We can't keep up with all the magazines and newspapers as it is."

I had to admit she was right. We get the *National Geographic*, and *Sunset*, and a number of others. I have a pile of *National Geographics* in the bathroom. *Sunset* is just the magazine to buy, if you want to build a gazebo, or a desert-style rock-garden, or cook Brussels sprouts in some daringly original way. I care to do none of these things, but the magazine comes anyway. And we get a local free newspaper, which has all the movie listings. It arrives on our doorstep every week. We also subscribe to the *San Jose Mercury* for some unknown reason. And the *Wall Street Journal* sporadically. So I let the *Chronicle* lapse. I was briefly pestered by telemarketers, but I held my ground firmly, and that was that. No further word— not at that point—about the death of Rupert Mobius. To tell the truth, I had forgotten all about it.

Later, when I was up to my neck in Mobius affairs, I went back and looked up the story in the *Chronicle*. I read it online. And then I printed out the story: "Elderly Man Killed in South of Market Apartment." It was fairly brief. Rupert Mobius, 84, was found dead in his apartment in a seedy neighborhood south of Market Street in San Francisco, shot to death. He lived alone. None of the other tenants had seen or heard anything. One tenant, a certain Fern Plotnick, who lived across the hall, may have heard a shot. At least according to this account.

The crime itself, alas, seemed all too ordinary. The police suspected it was the work of a burglar. Probably a drug addict. Everything is blamed nowadays on drug addicts. Much later, when I knew more about the death of Rupert Mobius, I learned that the police had in fact ruled out burglary quite early in the process. Nothing was stolen. Nothing of value, at any rate. Actually, Rupert Mobius had nothing much to steal. Not in his apartment at any rate. The shabby, run-down, junk-filled apartment was deceptive: Rupert Mobius, it turns out, was an extremely wealthy man.

The crime occurred in June. Late June. I entered the picture much later—October, in fact, when I had a phone call from a man who identified himself as Derek Mobius.

"Yes, Mr. Mobius," I said.

"You don't know me," he said. "But you handled my great-aunt's estate. Cassandra Hayden."

"Oh, yes. I remember that. What can I do for you?"

"My grandfather passed away a week ago. Simon Mobius. I'd like to talk to you about the estate."

"Of course."

Getting a new client was always welcome news. I made an appointment to see Derek Mobius the very next day.

But first I should tell you something about myself. My name is Frank May. I'm a lawyer in private practice, a member of the California bar. My office is in San Mateo, which as I said is a kind of suburb of San Francisco. San Francisco sits at the tip of a peninsula, with the ocean on one side and San Francisco Bay on the other. On the Bay side, it's suburb after suburb, all the way down to San Jose. San Mateo is one of these suburbs. It's firmly middle-class, with a nice downtown and a number of small office buildings full of dentists and the like. My office is in one of those buildings. My own dentist is across the street. I see him as rarely as possible.

I'm in my mid-40's, married—to Celia—and I have two teenage daughters. I'm in the general practice of law. I do small businesses and some real estate matters. But most of my work has to do with wills and trusts. I'm like a boatman on the River Styx. Only instead of people, I ferry money, assets, real estate, stocks and bonds, and everything a person can own, from the dead to the living, on the waters of death. I'm a kind of undertaker for money, taking over after the embalmers and the cremation people and the funeral parlors do their work. It's actually not a bad way to earn a living. I mean as a lawyer, not as an undertaker. I can't even picture the life of an undertaker. Or an embalmer. Or whatever you call somebody who cremates bodies.

I rather like what I do. It's a lot less lucrative than mergers and acquisitions, but the hours are better. And very much less stress.

Anyway, big firms in big cities do mergers and acquisitions. They're the whales in the legal sea. I'm something of a minnow. But a happy minnow. As I said, I do mostly estates work, but, in fact, I don't turn down business of any sort. Well, that's not exactly true. I would be tempted to turn down a patent matter, if a client brought one to me, but the client would have to be crazy to hire me in the first place. I don't know much about patent law, and you have to have a scientific mind. I have no such thing. Oh, yes: I don't like personal injury work, so I farm it out. And I don't like divorce, but I'll handle it in a pinch. Above all, I don't do criminal work. That's highly specialized, and besides, I don't want to get involved in such sordid matters. Burglars, drug lords: who needs that? Unfortunately, in a way criminal matters, as you will see, have a curious habit of pursuing me. The Mobius matter: there's a perfect example.

It began for me, as it turned out, with Derek Mobius and a question involving an estate. I do like to help people with what we call estate planning. Figure out what you want to do with your money, and I'll help you do it. Wills and trusts. And when you die—and we all do die—I'd love to handle your estate.

It's good clean work, mostly with families. Some of these are nice families, bourgeois families, with a house, a dog, children, rose bushes in the garden. Oh yes, and they have to have at least *some* money: otherwise it isn't worth my while or theirs. Some, as I say, are nice families. But even nice families have problems: maybe it's kids from two marriages, maybe the domestic situation is all screwed up, maybe there's a senile parent to be dealt with. Whatever. I've known many good families and also a number of crazy, dysfunctional families. But this story is about the Mobius clan, and they take the cake. Nobody could have invented such a weird and complicated story. It had everything, including, as it turned out, murder.

2

There I was, sitting in my office in downtown San Mateo, and young Derek Mobius sat across from me. We had just introduced ourselves and exchanged a few pleasantries. It was a chilly day in October—chilly, that is, by California standards. There was no sun, and the days were getting shorter.

Derek Mobius was a good-looking young man—in his mid-twenties, I would say—with dark blond hair, regular features, and a rather friendly smile. He was wearing a gray sweater and corduroy pants. He had a habit of running his fingers through his hair, as if to make sure it was still sitting on top of his head. Otherwise, there seemed to be nothing much about Derek Mobius that was strange or unusual.

He told me he was a law student at Stanford. Or had been: he had finished the first year and a half and then taken some sort of leave. "I'm getting my head together," he said. "I'll go back eventually."

I smiled. When I was in law school, I desperately wanted to quit. After two weeks, in fact. There was something mind-numbing about it. But I had paid my tuition already; and I couldn't see an alternative. A friend of mind told me: "You'll like it as soon as you get over your natural revulsion to the subject matter." He was basically right.

"As I said," he began, "I want to consult you about my grandfather's estate. His name was Simon Mobius. He died last week."

"I'm sorry to hear that."

"He had a heart condition. He was 82, I think. I don't know his exact age."

I tried to make sympathetic little noises. Then I said, "Tell me about his family. And, oh yes, did he have a will?"

"Yes, he had a will. But there's some... complications. I guess I should tell you more about the family. Simon—my grandfather—is a widower. Was, I mean. My grandmother died a long time ago. They had one child, a son, Piers Mobius. That was my father. He's dead, too, I'm afraid."

I expressed more sympathies. "No need to," he said. "You're my lawyer, so I'm supposed to be honest with you. I never knew my father. He died in an accident: he was on a small boat, a storm came up, and the boat tipped over or something. This was in the Pacific Ocean, somewhere off the coast of Australia. He lived in Australia. They never found the body. But no way could he have survived; and if he hadn't drowned right away, he'd be stuck there in the ocean, and nobody could have rescued him."

"When did this happen?"

"About a year and a half ago, maybe a bit more. As I said, I didn't know him at all. In fact, we didn't have much to do with the Mobius side of the family. Piers Mobius was not exactly father of the year. I'm sure he married mom because he got her pregnant. Not with me, but with my sister Doris. I came into the world a year later. According to my mom, he was never much on family responsibilities; he went off for days at a time when she was pregnant, and when the babies came, he didn't see any need to stick around. I mean, it was a household with two screaming children, diapers, and all the rest of that stuff. I had colic or something. Cried and cried. And Doris, she had some kind of rash. Anyway, my father, he just took off. That's when he went to Australia. I guess that was as far away from us as he could get and still speak English. My mother got a divorce. She never remarried."

"She's living, I assume."

"Mom? Oh yes, she sure is. Anyway, she raised us with a lot of help from her own family, especially Grandma Hayden. Mother's maiden name was Hayden. After the divorce, she went back to Hayden: Marylee Hayden. We were close to her and her family. It's funny: I'm a Mobius, that's my last name, but the Haydens were the only family I had. Except for Grampa Mobius—but when we were kids, he didn't loom very large in our lives."

"You say you never knew your father at all?"

"If I passed him on the street, I wouldn't recognize him. Oh, we had a few photos, but they're very old. And mother isn't exactly eager to display them. I don't even know where they are."

"And you never had any contact with your father?"

"Almost none. Every once in a while we did hear some news about him. Never good news. I mean, he was my father, but he was rotten to the core. That's what I heard. A con man basically, involved in all sorts of schemes. He seemed to be able to stay out of prison, I guess maybe he operated just this side of the law. And he was hardly living the life of a monk, if you get my drift. I heard he had at least two more wives, maybe three. Maybe he just walked out on all of them. No kids, though, as far as we know; but we're not really sure. Once or twice he sent us a Christmas card, one to me, one to Doris. I tore mine up, to tell you the truth. Doris... well, she had a different idea."

"A different idea?"

"My sister had a real hankering to connect with him. God knows why. One year she went on a trip to Australia, with a friend of hers, Justin. Justin always wanted to visit the Great Barrier Reef and go snorkeling, and that sort of thing. Doris: well she didn't mind reefs, but she really wanted to find our father. Supposedly he was living in

Brisbane at the time. The postcards came from Brisbane. Doris has a real sense of family. She's been tracing the Haydens, going way back, they were pioneers in Kansas, of all places. Anyway, before that they were in Rhode Island, and England; they came over from England. She's got tons of material from the census and what not. Amazing what you can find out these days."

"And... the Mobius side?"

"We know almost nothing. The only Mobius we knew was Grampa Mobius. We saw him once in a while, not often. Doris used to ask Grampa Mobius about his family background, but he never wanted to talk. He was a crotchety old man. Doris asked him questions about his ancestors, did they come from Germany, and when, and he'd say, well they're all dead, aren't they? Anyway: poor Doris went to Australia, and tried to find our dad."

"And did she?"

"No, not in the flesh. Oh, she heard plenty about him in and around Brisbane, none of it good. Anyway, people said he had gone away, or run away, whatever. There was some scandal about a young Filipina who was working in a bar. He was just plain gone. Nobody seemed to know where he was."

"Did he know she was in the country? His own daughter?"

"If he did know, he didn't exactly show any interest in seeing her. She thought she had finally figured out how to reach him, some ex-girlfriend of his hated him enough to give Doris a cellphone number. She actually called him, and he was not friendly, to be honest. What do you want from me, you know, that sort of thing. The ex-girlfriend said he had a drinking problem, a gambling problem, and he had a sex problem, too. He liked really young girls."

"And then he died."

"In a freak accident. Apparently he had some sort of boating license. God knows where he got it from, maybe he forged something. And he got some sort of job taking people for rides in these small boats. But then one night he went out on the boat himself, sort of a joy-ride. He had a new girlfriend—maybe weren't getting along. She was a piece of work herself, apparently with a criminal record. He had also gotten some fifteen-year-old pregnant. Anyway, he was on this boat, dead drunk—that was the rumor—and then this storm came, and that was the end of Piers Mobius. There was a huge stink about the fifteen-year-old because her father was some rich guy, maybe a politician. I think the kid had an abortion. Anyway, everything died down because old Piers was dead. Anyway, that was my father. My late father."

"So... your grandfather's heirs, that's you and your sister. Depending on what the will says, of course. You say he had a will, didn't you?"

"Sort of."

"Sort of? What does that mean?"

"I mean, he wrote it out himself. Is that legal?"

I said, "It can be if it's in his handwriting. We allow that in California."

"There aren't any witnesses. It's just a piece of paper. He didn't go to a lawyer."

"Doesn't matter," I said. "Do you have the will? I'd like to see it. And, by the way, are you supposed to be in charge? Did he name somebody as executor, the person who handles the estate, you know, manages it? You said your grandfather was a widower, didn't you?"

"Grandma died when we were very little. I guess I'm the closest living relative, along with my sister Doris. And the will doesn't say anything about any executor. Does that mean it's no good? "

"No, not really. The court can appoint somebody to take care of things."

"I guess that dumps the problem on me. Doris doesn't want to touch it with a ten-foot pole. She says, you had a year of law school, you do it. Hey, there's courses on that sort of thing, but not in the first year. But Doris didn't care; she wants me to do it. I'll do it, I suppose. I guess I have to. There's nobody else."

"And the estate.... What, uh, are the assets?" I asked. A perfectly normal, in fact an essential question. And one fraught with significance for *me* at least. My fees would depend on the size of the estate.

"Well, it's a bit complicated."

He had said that before. "Complicated? How so?" I asked. "Did your grandfather have money?"

"No. Nothing much. Social Security, and a couple of bank accounts. Maybe a few other things, nothing to speak of. But then recently he became very rich. At least potentially."

"Did he win the lottery? I mean, how come he ended up rich? And how rich?"

"Very rich," he said. "Millions, in fact."

It would have been both unprofessional and, worse, downright callous to rub my hands together with glee at this news, especially in front of a man who was telling me he had recently lost a close relative. Not that Derek Mobius seemed grief-stricken. But one had to act with the requisite proprieties. So I simply nodded, made a solemn face, and kept my smile to myself. And a good thing too, because my joy lasted only a few seconds, when Derek Mobius dropped his bombshell.

"I better mention the *real* complication," he said.

"OK. We lawyers, we're used to complications."

"But probably not this one," he said. "Grampa inherited his money from his brother, my Great-Uncle Rupert."

Rupert, Rupert. Rupert Mobius. The name rang a bell but only vaguely.

"And?"

"Uncle Rupert was murdered."

"That's terrible. How did it happen?"

"Not sure. But the police think it was Grampa who did it."

I was in shock. Not murder again! Murder seemed to

pursue me. What was it about me or my practice or my fate, that so many of my clients seemed to become enmeshed in some sordid murder thing? Then, suddenly, the synapses in my brain clicked, and I remembered the story I read in the *Chronicle*. The victim with the funny name. The murdered Mobius. That was Derek's great-uncle, as it turned out.

Derek went on: "We've got a neighbor, he's a lawyer, does mostly real estate, but he did tell me, you can't inherit if you killed somebody. So I can't help wondering, what would happen if it turned out, that my grampa *did* in fact kill his brother. I mean, it seems crazy. But Uncle Rupert is definitely dead, and somebody definitely did it. And if it was Grampa...."

"But, can I ask, why do you think your grandfather killed this man? And isn't this something, well, for the police?"

"For the police? Is it ever. And believe me, they were all over the place. And they were really after him, I mean, my grandfather. It was crazy. Questions, I mean, they were pretty persistent. You see, Grampa had visited his brother the day he died. And his fingerprints were all over the place—naturally. I mean, there was nothing sinister about that, was there? He told them his brother was alive when he left the house, but they didn't believe him. People saw him leaving the house, but so what? He admitted he had been to see his brother. But they were really on him, gathering evidence I guess or whatever they do."

"And then?"

"He had the last laugh. He fooled them. He up and died. A perfectly natural death: heart attack. He had a bad heart condition, longstanding problem. Anyway, he died; and I imagine that put an end to the investigation. I mean, I think it did."

"Because...?"

"Because, they were convinced that Grampa had been the murderer. And now that he was dead, well what was the point? I mean, maybe they were planning to arrest him or something. But you can't arrest somebody who's dead. So I have the feeling they decided, case closed; and they went on to other things. They've got plenty of murders and robberies to spend their time on. But my question is: if he did kill his brother, what then? Are we out of luck?"

I don't know the probate code by heart; it's hundreds of pages long. Clients seem unaware of this primal fact. I said to Derek, I thought that his inheritance was safe, but that I would have to check it out.

"In any event," I said, "let's assume your grandfather, uh, did this thing. And he's dead, and the case is closed. After all, if nobody objects to him or his family, I mean, objects to them inheriting, then there isn't a problem, is there?"

"Oh, but there is. Big problem. Cousin problem: my two cousins. Great-Uncle Rupert Mobius had two children, Katerina and Cranshaw. He basically cut them out of the will, left them next to nothing. And they're furious, as you can imagine. At least that's what I heard. The lawyer for my uncle's estate, he called me, and told me they were furious. I mean, he didn't use that language, but that was the message. I never met them, to tell you the truth, and I have no idea what they're like. But I suppose the old man must have had a good reason. I mean, you don't cut off your children unless they did something that really pissed you off. But, whatever. The point is, they're going to try to break the will, because that's their chance to get their hands on the money. I don't know what their case is. But if accusing Grampa helps their case, they'll certainly try to make that argument. Somebody told me they already hired a lawyer. So you see, it does make a difference, what happens, if this thing is pinned on Grampa."

Meanwhile, I reached behind me and took down from a shelf my trusty copy of the California Probate Code. Don't get me wrong: I am familiar with many of its dreary provisions. But as you can well imagine, in my day-to-day work, heirs who murder somebody who was going to leave them money—that doesn't come up that often. But I had very little trouble finding some answers to my questions. Yes, a person who "feloniously and intentionally" kills, cannot inherit from the deceased. Period.

"So that means your grandfather couldn't inherit," I said. "But that's not the question here. First of all, we haven't proven that he killed anybody, and maybe nobody will ever prove it. Second of all, he's dead. The question is, if he *did* kill his brother, and somebody can prove that, what does that do to *his* heirs? And frankly, I'm not sure. I'll have to do some checking." And then I added—because I don't like clients to feel I'm not totally up on the law— "Actually, it's a first for me. Most of my clients aren't accused of murder."

He looked puzzled, so I went on. "There's two options, legally speaking," I said. "Could be, it's treated as if the killer died before the guy he killed. That means, it's the same as if your uncle said, I leave my assets to my brother, and the brother died first. I'm pretty sure you and your sister would get your father's share. But the other option is, it cuts him off, along with everybody who would inherit through or from him. And that would be bad news."

"Well, what do these 'options,' as you call them, depend on?"

"State law," I said. "Each state is different. Don't worry, I'll check it out."

"I like option one," he said. "Naturally."

"Me too. Remember, it's not like he was arrested or anything like that. Of course all this is assuming a lot about your uncle's will. I wish we had a copy of it. You say that your cousins are contesting it. I'd have to know on what grounds. But—worst case—if they did succeed in breaking the will, well, that would be another story. You and your sister, frankly, would get nothing."

"Wow. Can they do that? I mean, get the whole will

thrown out?"

"Derek, I don't know. It's not easy to do, generally speaking; but some people do succeed. As I said, I'd have to know a lot more about the will, exactly what it said... and a lot more about your great-uncle, too."

"I told you, I hardly knew him. And I didn't even know my grampa all that well either."

I had a grandfather myself. Well, two of them, but one died before I was born. I tried to imagine my grandfather killing anybody, even my grandmother, who annoyed him a lot, but my imagination fell far short. Was the personality of Simon Mobius the key to all of this? I asked Derek to tell me about him.

"Well," Derek said, "Grampa Mobius lived most of his life in Fresno. I don't know what he was doing there. Some kind of job, I suppose. We hardly ever saw him. Mother didn't like him. She didn't like any of the Mobius family, and could you blame her? Anyway, we did drive there once, I remember, one summer, when Doris and I were kids. Have you ever been to Fresno?"

"Not really."

"It was so hot you could die. Honestly, that's what I remember most. He lived in this tiny house, and he was too cheap to turn on the air conditioner. He and his brother were both cheapskates. What a pair. Anyway, he wasn't exactly friendly, I guess because of mother; and of course, we were kids, and who wants to travel for hours and hours, just to see some crotchety old geezer? Anyway, my mom hated the whole family, like I said. But then, oh, maybe about five years ago, he got out of Fresno, and he moved to Mountain View. We live in Palo Alto, which is sort of next door to Mountain View. So we saw him once in a while. Grampa was a pretty weird old guy. He used to give us gifts at Christmas. Junk mostly. Things he bought at Goodwill, I swear. Once in a while, Mom said we ought to go see him. She wouldn't come, of course."

"Your father.... Did he have brothers and sisters?"

"No, he was an only child. Spoiled rotten, probably. It's a miracle anybody ever married Grampa Mobius, but some woman did. I never knew her: she died a long time ago. I think I told you that. Of course, who knows what he was like when he was younger. By the time he was living in Mountain View, he was almost a recluse—well, not literally, but kind of. He had a pension of some kind, a small one, and he got Social Security. And oh yes, he was some sort of religious fanatic. But not any organized religion, he despised them, a bunch of fakers he called them. He used to yell at us when we visited, why do you go to church, it poisons the mind, it's all lies. He was a believer, though, in some weird stuff. Later on, we found out, it was all because of his brother Rupert. I'll get to that. Anyway, Doris and I, we used to laugh about him and his ideas, we called it the Church of Mobius."

"But you did visit him."

"Well, occasionally," Derek said. "Doris... she hated going. She found him pretty repulsive. She said he smelled bad. Maybe he did, but I never noticed. Mind you, Doris is the one in our family who cares about relatives, ancestors, that sort of thing. I couldn't care less. Anyway, as I said, every once in a while, we would visit him. Mother even gritted her teeth and invited him over to the house, but he refused to come. Anyway, a few years ago, he called on the phone, and said he wanted to see me. That was pretty unusual, but I went. He told me about his will. He said, I'm getting old, I've got to think about such things. I want to tell you what I'm doing. I'm leaving it all to Piers. I know he's no good, he's over there in Australia, God knows what he's doing there, maybe he's screwing kangaroos, who knows. But he's my son, and he's the only one I've got. He said, he's the only person I ever loved, in my life. He's in Australia, and he might as well be dead for all the contact I have. But still, I love him."

"Go on."

"So he said, I want him to have my estate, Derek. You

don't need the money. You've got some money of your own, and I know you'll get money from the Haydens, they're stinking rich. Piers, well, that's another story. So I'm not leaving you anything. Doris neither. But I want you to manage the estate. You'll get a fee, so I'm not leaving you out altogether."

"And.... What did you say?"

"I said, fine, Grampa, you do what you want. We're not after your money. And in fact we weren't. Mom's family had some money, he was right about that, and when Grandma Hayden died, couple of years ago, Mom and her sisters inherited it. Grandma set up a trust, and Mom gets checks every once in a while. I don't know much about it. Some bank manages it. Anyway, Mom always had a good job with a software company, and they gave her stock, and stock options too. The point is, we were quite comfortable, the three of us. And anyway his will didn't matter—we didn't think about it at all, because we thought, who cares, he doesn't have any money. He was living in some little cottage in Mountain View behind a bigger house. And he always claimed he lived on his Social Security. He could have been lying, I suppose, but he certainly didn't *look* like he had any money, so what was the point of worrying about inheriting stuff he didn't have in the first place?"

I thought, what indeed was the point of it? I did think it was odd, an old miser living on Social Security, and talking about who would manage his estate. That was for rich people. Maybe he was just confused or had delusions of grandeur. Or else he was thinking of inheriting money himself—perhaps from his brother Rupert. But I didn't even dare think much along those lines.

Derek went on: "We knew vaguely about Grampa's brother Rupert, our great-uncle. I hardly knew him. Grampa mentioned him from time to time. He used to say why don't you visit your Uncle Rupert. He lives in San Francisco in some apartment. And I said sure, we will. But we never did. You know how these things are. One of the Hayden aunts lives in San Francisco, in a big housing development, Park Merced, and I never visited her either. Anyway, why would I want to see Rupert Mobius? What would I say to him? I had the impression that he and Grampa Mobius had not been particularly close for years. Maybe there was some family thing, some fight, but I guess that wasn't the case. Anyway, Grampa was living in Fresno for many years, so how could they see each other? Once Grampa came out here, they became really close. Uncle Rupert was older than Grampa, and he didn't get around much. Grampa used to go see him in San Francisco. He'd get on a bus and go up to the city. Rupert lived in the Mission District. Anyway, they were both widowers. Maybe they used to get together and complain about their worthless families. After my dad died, Grampa started going to see Uncle Rupert more. And then one day my mother said, you haven't seen or spoken to your grandfather, why don't you call him? So I did. I said, I could come see you some time. He said, sure—but not today, he said, he was going to visit his brother. That was the day Uncle Rupert got killed."

"And he did visit his brother; you told me he was there."

"He went and he came back. And then they found Rupert dead. Can you imagine? On that very day. And, bigger surprise, it turned out that old Rupert was very rich, I mean seriously rich. We knew he had some money, there were rumors. But nothing like what he really had. Maybe even a hundred million dollars. Blew my mind. He made it in real estate, he made it on the stock market, don't ask me how. And he was *really* a miser, lived in this miserable apartment, full of old newspapers piled up in a corner and turning all yellow, I mean, completely disgusting: dirt and filth everywhere, cobwebs, you name it. I'll bet there were roaches. Maybe rats, even."

Amazing. All that money, and cockroaches, too. It takes all kinds, as they say.

"Anyway, he used to eat mostly hamburgers from

McDonald's, cheapest thing he could get, or pizzas, with some kind of coupon he cut out of the newspaper. Whatever. At the end, he was practically living on Kellogg's Fruit Loops, or bran flakes; and, oh yes, jello, he loved jello; and he hardly ever went out of the house.... Maybe he was losing it by the time he died. But he had all this money. And he left it to *our* family, not his, can you imagine? He cut out his own children, and he left it to us. I can't imagine why. Well, they were brothers, and I guess blood is thicker than water—but to cut out his own children? Wow."

"So you have no idea why?"

"Beats me. He said something to my grampa about it, but it didn't make any sense. He said the 'spirits' told him to leave the money to my dad, who was his nephew. Mind you, my dad was already dead; and here the guy was leaving him millions of dollars. I think he had a screw loose. But I better not say that out loud."

I almost asked him—why not? But I quickly realized what the reason was. One screw loose might be OK, but too many, and the whole will might be imperiled.

"And if he was mentally incompetent, isn't that right, then the whole will is no good. And if that's the case, there goes the money."

"You say Rupert disinherited his children...."

"Yes he did. He had two kids—a son and a daughter. I have never seen them, but they are definitely in the picture."

"Where do they live?"

"No idea."

I could see this was going to get complicated. I had these visions, for a brief moment, of collecting a sweet fee for very little work; but now this fantasy was flying out the window. If there was an actual will contest.... Very few wills, you understand, are contested, and, to be perfectly honest, I have never had experience with one. Few lawyers who handle estates ever see a real will contest. I suppose they have to bring in a specialist: everything nowadays is specialists. I suppose there are doctors who have nothing to do with anything except the pancreas.

I kept my inexperience to myself. I asked Derek if he had a copy of his great-uncle's will. He did not. But he said he could get a copy, and I urged him to go ahead and do this. When I saw it, and read it, it was quite a shock. But that comes later.

3

The next few days I was involved in other work and had no occasion to spend my time thinking about the various members of the Mobius family. But then I had a call from a San Francisco lawyer who introduced himself as Gideon Grambling. Actually his secretary called, and told me, in a very self-important way, that Gideon Grambling was on the phone and would like to speak to Mr. Frank May, and was he available?

Grambling, whose voice oozed self-satisfaction—at least it sounded that way to me—announced that he was attorney for the estate of Rupert Mobius; he understood (he said) that I was attorney for the estate of Simon Mobius, and that he believed it would be useful for us to meet and discuss "various items concerning these two estates which are, as you know, interconnected." I agreed. He suggested that I come to his office in San Francisco. I would have preferred for him to come to my office in San Mateo; but it was clear from his very tone of voice that he considered himself the alpha male in this context, presumably because the money was all in the Rupert estate. Or it could have been because he was a big-time lawyer in a big-time city, which I was not. At any rate, I felt that I would have to learn how to live with Gideon Grambling, and it would not be necessary to *like* him to do that. I accepted his invitation to the city.

So I drove into San Francisco two days later for my appointment with Gideon Grambling. I live in a suburb of

San Francisco and my office is in another suburb; but it's surprising how rarely I go to "the City," which is what the locals rather arrogantly call it. Still, each time I go, I have to admit how seductive it is: the hills tumbling over each other, row on row of pastel-colored houses, the water on all sides, the cable cars, the tall buildings, the sunshine, the fog, the beautiful bridges. And the people on the streets, people from every race, every country; gaudy people, crazy people, homeless people pushing shopping carts, men in business suits, women in bright colors, hippies, drug addicts, billionaires. In some ways, it's a toy city, something out of a video game. There's something unreal about it, sort of made up and artificial. But people love it. Especially Europeans. They find it delightfully un-American.

I can understand this love affair with San Francisco. Particularly if you don't have to drive into town. If you do, you confront the dreaded parking situation. Parking is completely hopeless. And expensive. But I won't bore you with my parking troubles. Eventually, you always find a space. At enormous cost, to be sure. But I had allowed myself extra time, and I appeared at Grambling's office exactly when I said I would. That was possibly a mistake. Grambling, when I got to know him, struck me as the type who would interpret promptness as a sign of weakness. But perhaps I'm being unfair.

Grambling had a suite on the 14th floor of a sleek, new office building, all glass and steel, in the financial and legal area centered on Montgomery Street. He apparently had a partner, because the sign on the door said Grambling and Lombard, Attorneys at Law. The office was what I expected: excruciatingly modern furniture, a panoramic view, and an elegant reception area. Behind the desk sat a receptionist. She was beautifully coiffed, young but not too young—I'd say she was in her 40's—smartly dressed, and expensively, as far as I could tell. She had dyed blonde hair and extremely red fingernail polish. I told her who I was. She offered me tea or coffee while I waited, and (I imagine) announced my presence to Grambling.

I waited fifteen minutes or so, leafing through a magazine (the *Economist*), and then she showed me into Grambling's office. I wondered if the fifteen-minute wait was because he was busy with someone or something else, or was simply on principle. If you're shown right in, that might be a sign of weakness on *his* part, I suppose. Of course, if you make somebody wait *too* long, it's rude and unprofessional. Fifteen minutes or so in the outer office is just about ideal.

Grambling's office was large and elegant. Everything about it seemed calculated to impress: the view, which was even more spectacular than the receptionist's—I think he could see the Bay, the Golden Gate, the hills of Marin, and for all I know, the Sierra Nevadas. Then too, there was the Oriental rug on the floor, brilliantly colored and in sharp contrast to the ultra-modern chrome and leather of the furniture. There were tasteful paintings on the wall, abstract expressionist, but nothing offensive. Next to them was an ostentatiously framed diploma from Harvard Law School.

Most impressive of all was Grambling himself. He was tall and handsome, slightly bald, hair gray at the temples, but not too gray. He wore a dark suit, white shirt, and a quiet necktie. Not a hair was out of place. He was neither fat nor thin, but exactly right in the body-mass area. I'm sure he tended to his body the way a man might take care of a rare plant, or a tropical fish in a fishbowl. He looked almost too good to be true. I can't help wondering what people like him are really like. I mean really—underneath the façade. For instance, was he married or divorced? I guessed divorced. Somehow he *looked* divorced. I can't tell you why I thought so. In fact, as I found out later, he wasn't.

He shook my hand and introduced himself. He motioned me to a chair. Then he said, "I understand you're handling the Simon Mobius estate."

"I am."

"Let me give you some background," he said. "As you may know, my practice is restricted to estates and trusts, estate planning, and the like. It's a boutique practice, but if I may be permitted to say so, it's quite a flourishing practice. I have a reputation... and more clients than I can actually handle. I have one partner, Lily Lombard, and a paralegal of course. Our practice is restricted to... how shall I put it... to people in the upper strata of society. Substantial people with substantial estates. If I mentioned some names, which of course I won't do, you would recognize who they are. People in society. People in high positions, leaders in the tech industry, and so on."

I wondered why he was telling me these things, which seemed quite unnecessary--not to say obnoxious. It was obvious, unless he was some kind of con man, that Gideon Grambling did in fact have a very successful practice. I could only guess at what the rent for his office might come to. And I wondered what he would think of my own modest office or my own clientele, who were not "upper strata." Not that my clients are paupers. Frankly, if you're not well-off, you don't need the kind of services I provide. But of course, there's well-off, and then there's rich. And there's rich and there's super-rich. For Grambling, I suppose, you had to be super-rich. How else was he going to pay his exorbitant rent?

"This is necessary background," he said. "You see, when Rupert Mobius first came to see me, my receptionist had no intention of letting him come in to my office. Frankly, he looked like a homeless person: dressed in rags, I mean literally. She assumed he was looking for the key to the men's room, which of course we would never give him. These people, they come off the streets, they have an odor of course, and my clients don't like them, nor, to be frank, do I. Usually, they don't penetrate the 14th floor, as you can well imagine. Anyway, this man said to my receptionist that he knew about my work, and he wanted to see me. She said I was busy. Of course this was a lie, and he knew it. He insisted, he raised his voice, he said his broker had recommended me. Indeed he had; but I think the broker should have warned me what to expect. My receptionist thought: the man is delusional."

"But you did end up seeing him."

"Indeed. He was extremely persistent. I won't bore you with the details, but he mentioned some names, said something about his affairs. He finally managed to convince her that he was, in fact, a man of means and that he wanted to see me on legitimate business. May I ask, did you know Rupert Mobius?"

"Never had the pleasure."

"I can't say you were missing anything. He was not pleasant. He was also quite eccentric. Very, very strange. He had some, shall we say, *unconventional* ideas. In other ways, he was extremely shrewd, a hard bargainer—it's not hard to see why he was so successful, with his investments and his real estate. When it came to money, he knew exactly what he was doing and why. And when I explained legal technicalities, he caught on immediately. Many of my clients are, shall we say, deficient in that regard."

"And he wanted a will, I suppose?"

"Yes. Well, we discussed living trusts, and their advantages. You know, avoidance of probate costs, that sort of thing. And various other estate planning tools. He refused to even consider them. He was a very stubborn man. I told him we could save money for the estate, but that seemed not to interest him, compared to saving some money right now. 'I'll be dead,' he said, 'why should I care about probate costs?'"

"So you drafted a will."

"I did. A very odd will. In the first place, he told me he had two children, a son and a daughter, and he wanted to leave them virtually nothing. Disinherit his daughter totally, and leave a pittance to his son. Naturally, he had a perfect right to do that under the California Probate Code, as you well know. I gently suggested that perhaps that was not the wisest thing to do, and I began to explain why, but he was adamant. I had to assume that he knew what he was doing, and that he had good reasons to feel, uh, resentment against his children."

"Did he tell you why?"

"Oh, indeed. In great detail. I gather that his children tried to have him committed. At least that's what he told me. Or, failing that, to have some sort of conservator appointed. He was very bitter about this. They didn't succeed. Since then, he hasn't spoken to them, and has refused all contact. I must say, this is not the first time I've encountered this. Old people can be very sensitive. Conservatorships... I handle quite a few. Frankly, it's a delicate business. Very often it leads to a great deal of bitterness. A great deal."

I nodded. I'd had similar experiences.

He went on: "Rupert Mobius was, believe me, not an easy client. On fee matters, particularly. He constantly complained about my fee schedule, and suggested—can you imagine—that I might give him some sort of discount! I had to tell him point blank that my office was not a used car dealership or some Middle Eastern bazaar. He was welcome, I said, to try some other attorney. He would find that the better sort would never lower their fees, and when I made it clear that there were no bargains to be had in my office, he bowed to the inevitable."

"And then?"

"I drafted a will for him, according to his wishes. He took the draft and completely rewrote it. He brought it back to me. He had scrawled all over the hard copy I gave him to look over. Again we had a rather, shall we say, acrimonious session. In the end, of course, he is the client, and he can have what he wants, provided it's not against the law or totally absurd. I don't think he crossed that line, but he came close. At any rate, I want you to see a copy of the will. I explained to him why what he wanted was, well, not only unconventional, but in some ways improper. He told me in no uncertain terms that it had to be his way or no way. And it was clear that if I didn't do what he said, he would go to some other lawyer. I suppose I should have let him go, but as I said, he was the client after all."

And, I said to myself, he was a man with a huge estate, and the potential fees for his attorney would be more than enough to compensate for a little trouble from the client. Not to mention that dead people don't make trouble the way live people can.

"I've gone into all this detail," he said, "so you might have some understanding of this rather strange will. The unconventional language and the tone, and some of the provisions, are not the product of my office. By that I mean they were forced on me by Rupert Mobius. If you find parts of this will that are sensible, where the grammar is excellent, and the legal aspects prudent, you can be sure they're the product of this office. The rest is his. What else can I say."

He picked up the phone. "Ms. Guthrie, would you please bring in the Mobius file? Thank you." She appeared in a moment, and handed him a file. I noticed that she seemed to give Gideon an intense look as she transferred the file into his hands. It puzzled me for a second, and then I forgot all about it.

Gideon handed me a copy of the Mobius will.

I read it quickly. It was certainly unconventional. Weird, in fact. I tell my clients that wills are formal legal documents: they are not the place to write little essays or to express your emotions. I'm sure Gideon Grambling said something to that effect to Rupert Mobius, but it went in one ear and out the other. Take, for example, the clause where he disinherited his children. You can do that under American law, no problem, except in Louisiana. All you have to do is say so. You don't have to go into the reasons. But Rupert Mobius did:

"I have been bitterly disappointed in my children. Makes me wonder why people have children in the first place. My children are bloodsuckers. They want my money. They tried to put me in an insane asylum. They tried to get control of my money. Well, they failed. I leave my daughter Katerina the sum of $1, and I also leave $1 to any of her children living at the time of my death. Right now, she doesn't have any children, thank God. Anyway, $1 is more than she deserves.

"To my son Cranshaw, I leave $10,000. Cranshaw is a weakling, dominated by his sister. My advice is: take the money, and use it to get yourself a job. Make something of yourself. You had very little respect for me during my lifetime, under your sister's influence, I suppose. Well, so be it. I have no duty to support you after my death. And, Cranshaw, if you decide to contest this will, you can kiss the $10,000 goodbye as well. In the event of a will contest, I leave you exactly nothing."

"I see what you mean," I said to Gideon.

Gideon shook his head sadly. "I told him it wasn't a good idea. I said to him, you should keep such things out of your will. You are simply giving your children ammunition. They're going to claim you were a man of unsound mind; writing things of that sort doesn't help. He paid no attention. But do read on."

After this screed, a section followed in which Rupert Mobius actually disposed of his estate. He left half of it "to Fern Plotnick, my dear friend, in trust, however, for the charitable purposes hereinafter expressed. She is to procure a charter for a charitable foundation to be called the Mobius Fund for Psychic Research. Once the charter is procured, she is to become President of the Foundation. She is to name a Board of Trustees, which she will chair. I direct her to appoint the Reverend Elijah Foster-Morrison as Vice-President.

"The purpose of the Foundation is to pursue research on reincarnation, under the direction of the Board. The Foundation shall fund research into the transmigration of souls. It shall offer a prize of no less than $1,000,000, to anyone who demonstrates proof of reincarnation or who demonstrates that some creature, whether a human being or an animal, possesses the soul of a dead person. I also believe that it may be possible to demonstrate the existence of the soul. I believe that at the moment of physical death, the soul leaves the body; I desire the trust to offer a prize of no less than $500,000, to anyone who can prove the existence of the soul or who can show a photograph of the soul leaving or entering the body. I believe that modern cameras will be able to do this. In any event, no one is to serve on the Board who does not accept the premises on which the Foundation has been established."

I looked up at Gideon. "I assume you tried to talk him out of this foundation idea, too."

"Of course I did. It's not going to be easy to get the IRS to recognize it as a charity, but I'm going to have to try. Not to mention a host of other problems. And, oh Lord, leaving control to Fern Plotnick...."

"May I ask, who is she?"

"She's an elderly widow, a neighbor of Rupert Mobius. Lived in the same building. She was his closest friend, I believe. I'm not sure friend is the right word. I'm not implying anything romantic. He was a very old man, and when you meet Ms. Plotnick, you'll understand why I rule out anything but a sort of colleagueship, although of course there's no accounting for tastes. In any event, they had a lot in common. I think many of these notions came from her. Or they worked them out together. I've spoken to her. She's completely unqualified to serve as executor or trustee. Completely. But it's not clear what we can do about that. She's a very peculiar woman, but I can't say that she's legally insane, and it wouldn't be easy to remove her from office."

The other half of the estate was also left to Fern Plotnick, as trustee of a trust, which the will called the Mobius Family Trust. This part was drafted with the heavy but no doubt accurate hand of Gideon Grambling. I'll spare you the legal jargon. The basic plan was simple. Income from this trust would be paid to Piers Mobius, the testator's nephew, for as long as Piers was alive. Piers, however, also had the right to terminate the trust at any point, and simply take over his half of the estate—a tidy sum of money. I paused in my reading: "But Piers of course is dead. He drowned: a boating accident. Wasn't Rupert Mobius aware of this?"

"He most certainly was. Just read on," he said.

On the death of Piers Mobius, according to the will, if Piers had not ended the trust and taken all the assets for himself, the trust would come to an end and the assets would be distributed to the testator's brother, Simon Mobius, if living. If he was not then living, then it was to be divided equally among those children of Piers Mobius who were living at the death of the last of the three to die of Rupert, Simon, and Piers Mobius. I more or less knew about this part of the will already. Grambling had informed Derek and his sister, and they were positively salivating over the money. There was however a condition attached, and it was about as weird as weird can be. We'll get to that in a minute.

"Well," Derek had said to me. "All three of them are dead, right? Grampa, my father, and Uncle Rupert. So the money comes to Doris and me, as soon as the estate is settled. And it's a lot of money. I wormed the information out of that lawyer—what a creep he is—but in the end he told me that, after taxes and expenses and whatever, he thinks there's some forty million dollars there, in that half of the estate. Can you imagine? And the man was living in that rat-infested slum, and eating bran flakes and jello. Forty million dollars. Doris and I would each get about twenty million dollars, maybe less because of taxes, but anyway, wow, that's a lot of money."

"Wow" was right. Twenty million dollars *is* a lot of money. Some of the billionaires here in Silicon Valley might consider it lunch money, but for the rest of us, it's serious coin. Derek and Doris were very likely going to be rich. The more Derek thought about it, the more excited he got. At our first meeting, he had been somewhat restrained. But after, when I spoke to him over the phone, he struck a very different chord. He seemed drunk with the heady odor of money. He said, "Wow. That money. I mean, I could kiss law school goodbye. I hate the place. I don't belong there. Bunch of creeps, students and professors. The stuff you have to read, it's so boring you could cry. And they call on you in class! You'd think you were back in high school. Man, I could start a business with the money. This is Silicon Valley. I could start a company: I wouldn't even need venture capital. I'd have a website. I've got some ideas. Oh, I could do all sorts of things. Travel. Go first class to Paris. I'd be rich."

Of course, it wasn't quite that simple, as I explained to him, over and over. There was a legal obstacle to overcome: there was, first of all, the question of the murder. If Simon Mobius had killed his brother, I think Derek and Doris would still be all right; but this was by no means certain.

Who did kill Rupert Mobius? I had no idea. A lot of people had a wonderful motive. Money is the motive of motives. Quite a few people would have gained financially if they killed the old goat. Simon, of course. But his grandchildren also. And perhaps Fern Plotnick? Or Rupert's own children? That was a little harder to see. Did they know they were disinherited? Or maybe they just hated the old man.

I had another thought, one that brought a smile to my face. How about Gideon as a murderer? Old Mobius was a colossal pain in the ass, and he was worth much more dead than alive. I loved the thought of Gideon as a murderer. I loved conjuring up an image of Gideon in handcuffs and an orange jumpsuit. Stabbing trash on the side of the freeway with his peers. The thought gave me intense satisfaction.

An even greater obstacle faced Derek and Doris. Suppose a court decided Rupert "lacked testamentary capacity," as the phrase goes, meaning in plain English that the will was no good, because the old man was a lunatic.

Katerina and Cranshaw Mobius would push that line as hard as they could. After all, if the will failed, the old man's estate would go to his next of kin. Katerina and Cranshaw. Usually attacks on wills do not work, but once in a while they do. And in this case, considering who the old man was, and the way he acted....

All these thoughts flashed through my mind. Meanwhile, I continued reading the will. The next few paragraphs were truly bizarre. I'll quote some passages verbatim:

"I have made elaborate provision for my nephew, Piers Mobius. It is reported that Piers Mobius is dead. But I believe that death is not an absolute. I believe that all of us have a soul as well as a body. I believe that there is a state of being in which the body may be dead, but the soul remains alive. I believe that there are conditions, too, in which the body is neither dead nor alive. I believe that my nephew, Piers Mobius, has passed into a kind of intermediate state. I have had visions in which I have seen my said nephew, and I believe that souls in that intermediate state can return and resume their life. I have had actual messages from my nephew, Piers, from the beyond. They have been conveyed to me directly, and through the intervention of Fern Plotnick, who can confirm this.

"If Piers Mobius returns from the dead within a reasonable time, he may claim the estate. It is immaterial to me what form his return may take. It is unlikely that he will return in the exact bodily form that he occupied during his stay here on Earth. I believe in reincarnation. I have read many things about the Dalai Lama; I have studied the process whereby a new Dalai Lama is chosen. Indeed, Piers Mobius, if he returns, will perhaps take the form of a little child, a newborn child. And we will be able to recognize this child through the science of genetics. We do not have to resort to guesswork. Sometimes when a child is born, the spirit of some dead person inhabits the soul of that child. I believe that within a year or so, we will have evidence of the return of Piers Mobius, and I believe that it may take the form of a newborn child. In that case, it is my will that that child shall inherit the share of my estate which I have left to Piers Mobius."

The man was completely out of his mind, I thought to myself. Little did I know that, in a very short time, I would have to think again about Rupert's rather deviant notion of reincarnation. You will see what I mean, in due course. But at the time, it simply struck me as ridiculous.

"I've been in this business for twenty years," Gideon said, "and I've never seen anything so absurd. I had half a mind to wash my hands of the whole matter. But if you read on in the will, you'll see that Mobius names me as attorney for the estate, and appoints Ms. Plotnick executor. Of course, I *could* withdraw as attorney, but perhaps it wouldn't be quite appropriate. I haven't made up my mind as yet."

He didn't fool me for a moment. Yes, the estate would be a colossal headache, no question. But it was a very large estate, and his fees were also potentially quite large. At least he had the decency not to say anything about his duty to the estate, or any twaddle of that sort. He was in it for the money, no question.

"He also names a successor executor and trustee: the Reverend Elijah Foster-Morrison. He was mentioned also in connection with the foundation. I've never met the man."

"Is he another neighbor?"

"No, not at all. He's some sort of fake, runs something called the Church of Divine Wisdom: I did a bit of investigating. He is, shall we say, not exactly the traditional sort of religious figure. His background is obscure, to say the least. He's originally from Cincinnati, and his actual name was Herman Schwartz. I have the impression that before he found religion—or one might say, before he founded a religion—he was a real estate broker of somewhat dubious morality. But it's not for me to judge."

It was certainly an odd will, an eccentric will. Hopefully, not *so* eccentric that Katerina and Cranshaw would win and have the will thrown out. My own duty was plain. My client was Derek Mobius and his grandfather's estate—and his sister was a client too, I suppose. I was not directly involved in the estate of the late Rupert Mobius. That was, in the main, Gideon's affair and his headache. But it had a direct impact on my clients. And thus on my fee.

In many ways, all I could do was wait and see. Gideon would have the pleasure of sorting out all the ins and outs of the estate of Rupert Mobius.

As far as the will of Simon Mobius, it was simplicity itself. It was a homemade will, written in a scratchy and spidery hand, on a plain piece of paper, and stuck into an envelope which Simon had sealed, and on which he wrote: "This contains my will." In the will itself, he left everything to his grandchildren. The will was dated and, as far as I could see, was a perfectly valid example of what we in California call a holographic will. It was a fairly recent will. Simon had told Derek he was leaving everything to his son Piers, but Piers was dead, and Simon obviously thought he needed a new will, which is what this was.

I checked with Derek and Doris. They expressed no doubt that it was genuine and that this was their grandfather's writing. "Grampa mentioned it to me once," Derek said. Doris fished out from somewhere a Christmas card he had sent. It was a cheap, hideous card, which probably had retailed for 99 cents. Old Mobius had signed his name and appended some platitudinous words. The handwriting certainly looked like the writing in the will.

I filed the will in the local Probate Court. As I did so, I couldn't help wondering what would happen next. Was this going to be a windfall for me or a colossal pain in the butt? Or both. You will see how it turns out in the end. I'll only say this: the path had many twists and turns and many surprises. Dead men tell no tales, but they can sometimes do surprising things. Or seem to. Wait and see.

4

I was busy the next few days, absorbed with my clients and their troubles, big and small. I spent very little time on the Mobius estate. Not that there was much to do. I had, as I said, filed the will of Simon Mobius in probate court. There was no trouble getting the will admitted to probate and arranging for Derek to be administrator of the estate. All very routine. The real action, of course, concerned Rupert, not Simon. That estate and that will was clearly a complicated mess.

Gideon called me one Thursday afternoon. He was planning, he said, to get the major players together in conference. He wanted me to be there, along with Derek and Doris, the two (apparent) heirs, and Fern Plotnick as well. I was of course eager to meet this woman. The conference was set for the following Monday, that is, if Derek, Doris, and I were available. As it turned out, all of us could make it.

That Monday was a gray foggy day in San Francisco. San Francisco has many of these days. People in the East who are not familiar with our area sometimes imagine it as some sort of tropical paradise. It's not. I should add, though, that my town, down the peninsula, has much better weather than The City. Less fog, for one thing. Often you can see the fog, hanging over the tops of the mountains that separate us from the Pacific Ocean. It's a mass of dense clouds, but, fortunately, it has the decency to stay away from the bay side of the peninsula, for the most part.

I arrived somewhat late. An accident on Highway 101 had caused a traffic jam, so I imagined (correctly) that I would be the last to arrive. I came to Gideon's office in a somewhat breathless state. The receptionist, Ms. Guthrie, gave me a disapproving look (or was I imagining that?) and ushered me into a pretentious conference room. It had a huge glass window, sleek furniture, and on the floor, a thick rug, in dramatic black, white and grey, that shouted out: look at me, I'm terrifically expensive. In the middle was a large table covered with glass, screens and other paraphernalia for video-conferencing and other modern miracles.

They were all there already, sitting around the table. Gideon seemed extremely annoyed, and looked ostentatiously at his watch. I made my excuses. I'm sure he thought I was lying.

You've met Derek of course. Doris, his sister, resembled him, but was a bit heavier. She had thick blonde hair which she was probably not born with (the color, I mean), and she wore a little too much makeup for my taste. But that doesn't matter.

It was Fern Plotnick that I was most interested in. She was, I'd say, in her late 60's or early 70's: it was hard to tell. She was decidedly overweight and her stomach bulged out. If she was thirty years younger, I would have thought she might be pregnant. On the other hand, she was extremely flat-chested, or so it appeared. She had very curly gray hair which tumbled over her shoulders, looking unkempt and, frankly, rather dirty. I don't normally notice what people are wearing—Celia is much more acute about such things—but in the case of Fern Plotnick, it was hard not to notice. Her skirt came just past her knees; underneath, there were ugly yellowish stockings of some sort. Probably the kind you wear when your natural-born veins are not up to the job. It would be churlish, I suppose, to hold that against her. More to the point, her shoes were scuffed, ugly, unfashionable, and needed a shine. The skirt... well, I can't quite describe it. A one word description might be *hideous*. It was somehow shapeless and nondescript. Her blouse had some sort of faded floral print. It was half tucked into her skirt, half hanging down. It was also quite wrinkled. If there's a fashion magazine for bag ladies, she would be the cover girl. She kept biting her fingernails during the conference, which I found both distracting and mildly repulsive. She had very dark eyes, deep-set, and a cleft double chin. She had a way of staring that was extremely disconcerting. You wondered: what on earth is going on in her mind? And I couldn't help thinking: this woman is supposed to manage a huge estate? That seemed clearly impossible.

Gideon sat at the head of the long conference table. He cleared his throat, indicating that the meeting was about to begin. He intoned: "I believe you know why you are all here. I am, as you know, attorney for the estate of Rupert Mobius. You have all been provided with copies of the will, and I presume that you have made yourself acquainted with it... and with its, shall we say, unconventional provisions. Simon Mobius, brother of the deceased, was one of the heirs. Simon Mobius is now himself deceased, as you know. You, Derek, and you, Doris, are his closest living relatives. Under the will, a trust was created, and the income was to be paid to Simon Mobius, as long as he lived. The estate promises to be a contentious one, and the trust was never, in fact, set up, in the short space of time before Simon Mobius died. However, the estate has earned considerable income, which, under the will would have gone to Simon Mobius."

"Income? How much income?" Derek asked. "And who gets it?"

"I don't have the exact amount. Perhaps $100,000. This accrued income will be paid into the estate of Simon Mobius. Of course, there are elements of uncertainty, and I am afraid there may be considerable delay. There are, shall we say, legal difficulties. There is, to begin with, the strange way in which Rupert Mobius met his death."

"Why is that relevant?" Derek asked. Of course, he knew the answer; we had talked about it. I supposed he wanted to hear it from Gideon.

"Well, a certain amount of suspicion has fallen on your late grandfather...."

"And does that matter?"

"That remains to be seen. Perhaps not. There is of course another question. It is a very odd will, and Rupert Mobius was a very unconventional person. His children, who were disinherited, have engaged a lawyer and they are planning to contest the will."

"Do they have a case?" Doris asked.

"In my judgment they do not," Gideon said. "But with regard to such matters, it's difficult to be certain. They are claiming, in the first place, that Rupert Mobius was not competent to make a will. That he lacked the capacity... because of, uh, mental illness and the like. In particular, they claim that he had delusions, hallucinations.... It's not a strong case, but I would hate to have to go before a jury. This is because the will is what the literature calls, rather quaintly, an 'unnatural will.'"

"Unnatural?" Doris asked.

"Let's just say that it's a technical term. It is presumed to be unnatural to disinherit your children. And it certainly isn't common. But we can show that he had his reasons. Nonetheless, an unnatural will is, shall we say, a bit more vulnerable than ordinary wills."

"Vulnerable?" Doris said.

"I mean, the chances of success in this lawsuit, the one against the estate, is at least marginally higher than it would otherwise be. And, oh yes, the children, the ones who are contesting the will, are also alleging undue influence. Let me explain that rather strange legal concept. The basic idea is that someone, well, exerted such power over the deceased that in a sense the will is not really his own."

"Someone?"

Gideon seemed a mite embarrassed. "The allegation," he said, clearing his throat, "is that this, uh, influence came from Fern Plotnick."

We all looked at her. She had been sitting silently up to this point. From time to time, she rocked her body a bit on her chair. At other times, she seemed to be staring out the window. I wondered how much of all this she was taking in. Now, for the first time, she spoke: she nodded her head from side to side, as if to show disapproval of these goings-on, and then she said, in a low and hoarse voice, practically a whisper: "Rupert will be very angry."

"Pardon me?" Gideon said.

"I said Rupert will be very angry."

"Rupert?"

All of us were startled, of course. Dead men do not get angry.

She went on, nonchalantly. "Yes, Rupert. He's watching everything we're doing. And he's very, very angry. I can feel it inside."

I'm sure the four of us were all thinking the same thing: this woman is out of her mind. I asked myself once more how she would manage an estate of eighty million, or a hundred million, or whatever it turned out to be worth. Appointing Fern Plotnick executor and trustee: that fact alone cast some doubt on the mental condition of the late Rupert Mobius.

Fern would be mainly Gideon's problem, of course. He was going to have to deal with her. Somehow. Indirectly, though, it was going to be mine as well: my clients, after all, were important heirs of Rupert Mobius, now that their father was dead. And Fern was executor and trustee of the estate. I had to hope Gideon could somehow succeed in controlling her. Or, best of all, getting rid of her as trustee and executor. I had the feeling that would not be an easy job.

5

Before heading for home, I had coffee with Derek and Doris. They both seemed to be extremely eager to get money out of their uncle's estate. I suppose this was only human on their part. I don't think either of them was particularly mercenary. But the thought of millions of dollars hanging on the tree just beyond their immediate reach, was intensely intoxicating. Adam and Eve couldn't resist low-hanging fruit either.

Doris, who struck me on the whole as a woman of common sense, energy, and integrity, was positively intoxicated by the prospect. "Imagine," she said, "there's $50,000 for each of us already, and we can't get it because of two greedy bastards."

"Hey, Doris," Derek said in a joking tone, "you're talking about our cousins."

"Cousins indeed. We never met them in our life. Who needs them? And they're standing between us and the money. The old man must have had a reason to cut them off. Anyway, I think it's a disgrace to claim your own father was incompetent, just to get your hands on the money."

"It's an awful lot of money," I said. "People do all sorts of things for money." They do. Of course, I was thinking: all sorts of things, including murder. But I didn't say this out loud. Instead, I tried to talk calmly to them. I suggested that maybe the worst could be avoided, maybe there could be some sort of settlement with

Katerina and Cranshaw.

"They don't deserve a dime," she said.

"Well, we don't either, Dodo," Derek said. "Dodo" was obviously his nickname for his sister. No doubt she hated it. "We had nothing to do with the old geezer, and now we're in line for all of his ill-gotten gains."

"It's so frustrating," she said. "And who knows what's to become of the money anyway, with that total wackjob in charge."

"Can we get rid of her, Frank?" Derek asked.

"Not so easy," I said. "But maybe Gideon can persuade her to back down."

I had my doubts about that. Still, it was probably worth a try. Dodo and Derek were becoming excited at the thought of inheriting a lot of money, and Gideon and I were getting equally excited at the thought of the fees. It would be downright criminal to lose all of that to Katerina and Cranshaw. Would Gideon try to settle with them? If it came to that, I would have to be involved too, I suppose.

I said goodbye to my clients and walked to my car. As I was getting ready to pay the exorbitant parking fee, my cellphone rang. It was Gideon. "I just had a call I think you ought to know about," he said. "It was from this Reverend Elijah person."

"And?"

"As you know, he is the successor trustee and executor, under the will. He had the colossal gall to suggest that we join forces to get rid of Fern Plotnick. As executor and trustee. 'She's a member of my flock,' he said, 'and of course she is very dear to me. But she's a woman of great delicacy and sensitivity, and I feel a task of this sort would be far too much of a strain. It would be best, of course, if she stepped down.'"

"And how was this supposed to be accomplished?"

"He said he would give her pastoral advice, and he wanted my 'moral support,' as he put it, 'if not legal support.' Of course I refused. But we haven't heard the last of him."

We agreed that it would indeed be best if Fern Plotnick was relieved of her duties as executor and trustee. "It's not just that she is woefully ignorant of such matters," Gideon said. "Many of our clients are naïve and untrained in legal matters. But they are willing to *listen* and willing to let me guide them. Ms. Plotnick, I am afraid, has a mind of her own. Insofar as she has a mind at all."

"Oh yes, one more thing," he added. "Katerina and Cranshaw Mobius are quite serious about contesting the will. They've retained a Palo Alto lawyer, a woman named Lisbeth Oaks. Do you know her?"

"Yes, slightly," I said. She was an older woman, as I recalled. A solo practitioner. She had been with a law firm once, in San Francisco, but for some reason left them and went out on her own. She did mostly family law—a euphemism for divorce—and as far as I know had never handled a will contest. But then neither had I. A thousand wills and no will contests. I also vaguely remembered that Lisbeth Oaks had a husband, somebody who did something or other with computers, and that his name was Judd. I decided to reach out to her and find out what, if anything, was happening. So I called her and said, "Hi Lisbeth, how are things going?"

"Oh, comme çi, comme ça. I'm surviving."

"And, uh, Judd, how's he?"

"Rotten, I hope. We're divorced. He found greener pastures. Good riddance."

I had no comeback for that one, snappy or otherwise, so I switched quickly to the business at hand. "You're representing Katerina and Cranshaw Mobius, I heard."

"You heard correctly."

"And you're contesting the will...."

"We are. I know what you're going to say. No, I don't have any experience with will contests. We've engaged a specialist, Arpad Sheckley."

"OK. I'm handling the estate of their uncle, Simon Mobius; he was one of the heirs of the estate of his brother, Rupert Mobius."

"Yes, assuming the will stands. But you know that, Frank. So get to the point."

"Shouldn't we get together? Talk this over?"

"I suppose. But why? What are you thinking about? Not some sort of settlement. It's not up to you, after all. It's that stiff Gideon whatever-his-name, he's the one."

"I know that, Lisbeth. I wasn't born yesterday."

"Neither was I. Look, Frank: I was actually going to call you. My clients, Katerina and Cranshaw, have so far absolutely refused even to think about a settlement. And they expressed a desire, for some reason, to meet with you and your clients. They want to get to know their cousins, they said. Apparently they've never met. I advised them against it. Your interests are adverse, to put it mildly. But they insist at least on seeing *you*, for some unknown reason. Would you be willing to meet with them?"

Why me? But I was curious to meet them. I said: "Sure, if my clients don't object."

"If your clients are like the rest of the family, who knows what they'll do. But never mind. I'll tell my clients to call, unless I hear otherwise from you."

I made doubly sure that Lisbeth was authorizing this. It would be a major ethical no-no for me to talk to her clients directly, unless she "consented," under a rule that I think was invented mainly to keep clients from shopping around for new attorneys or settling cases to cut their lawyers out. And even with permission, it was rarely well advised. Talk about an ethical Pandora's Box. But I was too curious to hide behind Rule 2-100 of the California Rules of Professional Conduct and pass this meeting up.

6

I spoke on the phone to Derek, who thought it was puzzling too; he said he'd talk to Doris. He called back and said she had no objection. Sure enough, a day later a woman called, announced she was Katerina Mobius, and would I have time to meet with her and her brother, Cranshaw? We set up an appointment.

Before they came, I made some discreet inquiries about these two. Gideon was the source of a good deal of information about them. Katerina was the older of the siblings. She had been married two or three times, each time ending in divorce. Gideon thought there were children somewhere, but he wasn't sure. In any event, she did not have custody of whatever children might have come out of these marriages; perhaps they were over 18. She had lived in Vermont for a number of years, where she was involved in some sort of business that sold wood-burning ovens. The business apparently failed. Then she tried to make money by writing a maple syrup recipe book. It was published by a vanity press and sold 36 copies. After the last divorce, she moved back to California, where she shared an apartment in Cupertino with her brother Cranshaw. She seemed to have some sort of job; Gideon wasn't sure what it was.

There was not much to say about Cranshaw. He had been married once, for about three months. The marriage was annulled. No children. According to Gideon, his sister was the dominant figure of the two. Cranshaw had dabbled in real estate, it seemed, with money his mother had left him. Mostly houses in Atherton, a very upscale market. But when the real estate market tanked, he lost most of his money. He was currently unemployed.

Now the two of them were sitting in front of me. Cranshaw Mobius was a man of about 40, cadaverously thin, with a long neck and bloodshot eyes. He was wearing a wrinkled white shirt and a yellow tie with blue polka dots. He had a very prominent Adam's apple and very skinny, bony fingers. His palm felt clammy and wet when we shook hands. I resisted the urge to squirt some disinfectant on my fingers.

"I'm between situations," he told me.

His sister did most of the talking. Cranshaw for the most part simply nodded his head as she spoke, and his Adam's apple bobbed up and down.

Katerina Mobius resembled her brother in many ways: she was also quite thin and bony, with a long neck, and sharp gray eyes. She was older than her brother; I would guess she was about 50 or so. She was wearing a black skirt and a blue blouse. Like Doris, she had dyed hair; but in her case, it was dyed dark black, the color of shoe polish. Older women, for some reason that escapes me, thinks this makes them look young and beautiful. They treat gray hair as if it's some sort of loathsome disease. Celia is turning gray, and I find it very attractive. Maybe I should say silver, instead of gray.

"We were not on good terms with our father," Katerina said. "He resented us, and he was really angry because we were trying to have a conservator appointed. But we only wanted to protect him, to help him, out of love. Of course, he thought.... Well, you know what he thought. Really, though, it had become absolutely necessary, because he was a sick man. His behavior... and the place he lived in: it was disgusting."

"Nauseating," Cranshaw said.

"And that woman, that Fern person; she would have

taken every last penny. I swear it. Anything *she* didn't take would go to that fake Reverend. And it was really *our* money. I mean, ethically. He was our father. Doesn't that count for something?"

Cranshaw nodded dutifully.

Katerina went on: "That woman, she's a parasite. I believe she was taking money from him. He was vulnerable. You know, old people are. That was father. Just the kind that would fall prey to a leech, a disgusting woman." She wiped a tear off her face. "Taking his money. And filling his head full of nonsense, crazy stuff."

Cranshaw nodded again.

"And the Reverend too.... Vultures, that's what they were. I mean, we'd been waiting a long time. Does that shock you? Not that we were just waiting for him to die, waiting for the money. No, that's not it at all. But we did have certain, well, expectations. And we deserved them. If I told you the whole story, the life we led, growing up, with that man. Mother was so sweet. She was like a little mouse. He dominated her. Totally. Shouted at her constantly. So demanding. I think he hounded her to death."

"Poor mother," Cranshaw said.

"He was a sick man! A sick man!" Katerina said. "A miser. The richer he got, the more of a miser he was. He wouldn't pay for our college. He said, you better make your own money. Cranshaw wanted to make something of himself, didn't you, Cranshaw?" (More nodding). "But no, it wasn't in the cards. And my brother, he's not the healthiest person, he's had asthma all his life. No, no college for us, unless we worked our fingers to the bone. I wanted to be a nurse, go to nursing school, but it was out of the question."

"Mother tried to help," Cranshaw said, and seemed almost on the verge of tears.

"But what could she do?" Katerina cried out, almost shouting. "She was under his thumb! She had money from Grandma when she died, but he controlled it, every penny. My dear mother used to sneak out to buy me some clothes on the sly. She was scared to death of him, though, scared he'd find out. And the abuse we took...."

"Abuse?" I asked.

"Oh, I don't mean physical.... It was mental abuse. Yelling, screaming, calling us lazy, good-for-nothing. Even when we were grown. He always thought it was only about the money. He didn't realize that *we* had a sense of duty, even if *he* didn't. After all, he *was* our father, the only one we had, and after Mother died, well, we felt we had to look after him, didn't we, Cranshaw?"

Cranshaw nodded, and the Adam's apple bobbed up and down quite violently.

"And we did try. We tried and tried, but it wasn't easy. That place! I mean, the roaches! Thank God I didn't see rats, I think I would have fainted if I had. Did you know he had a house once, we grew up in a regular house, in Fremont. It wasn't a great house, but it was a house. He sold it after Mother died. Made money on it, a big profit—the housing market was insane. He always made money. That's all he was good for, making money. And then he moved into this place. We couldn't believe it. When he sold the house, we said, Dad, what about us, where will we live, this is our home. He said he didn't care, that we were on our own. I'm not giving you handouts, he said. You're grown-ups. And then he moved into this awful place. Cranshaw and I, we had to rent an apartment ourselves. Mother left us a little money. And when we went to see him, the two of us, we were shocked. We said, Father, how can you live in a place like this?"

"That's what we said," Cranshaw said, in a kind of echo.

"Did he appreciate our concern? No, he was always suspicious: all you want is money money money, he would say. Of course we didn't want the money," she said, wiping away a tear. "Oh, the money would be useful, I won't deny that. But we just wanted to be a family. We said, Dad, we'll get a nice place, we'll all three of us live together. Oh no, he said, you just want to sponge off me. That's what he said! Am I right, Cranshaw?"

"Yes, he said that."

"That really hurt. And I said to him, Father, you can't live like this. He said, I'll do as I damn please. The rent was cheap, that was the whole attraction. And when I came, I always saw him with that Plotnick woman. She was there night and day. I'm not saying she slept there, I'm not saying there was any sexual thing, as far as I know.... I mean, our father was *old* and she didn't seem like the type. But I could see she was dominating him, really. It was the money, I'm sure. She smelled the money. And that's why we decided, reluctantly, this has got to end, we have to take control. We went to a lawyer.... And the lawyer, Henry Finchley, do you know him? San Francisco?"

I did not, I told her

"Well, he recommended this conservator thing. Father was becoming more and more irrational, that's the gospel truth. And the woman was dominating him. So we filed these papers. Finchley said it was a sure thing, but it wasn't. Father was so angry, so bitter, and he had all these high-priced lawyers, and he won the case. I'm sure they got to the judge, what else could it be? You know the rest. He refused to see us after that. His own children."

More tears.

"We're through with Finchley," she said, when she had recovered her composure. "We have a new lawyer now, two of them, in fact. Lisbeth... I believe you know her. She will handle our case for the most part, and we have another lawyer too, a specialist named Arpad Sheckley, he's going to handle the actual will contest. Lisbeth really hasn't ever done that sort of thing. They say he's very good, he's broken tons of wills. We have a *very strong* case: he told us that. On the grounds of lack of capacity, that's the phrase. Father was in no condition to go making out wills, not in his mental state, and not with that woman around. Arpad said he thought we could win."

"Those cases are difficult," I said carefully. I had never heard of Sheckley. I doubted whether he had "broken tons of wills." Will contests are rare and they usually lose. This one seemed particularly chancy.

"Arpad said," she went on, "that we have a good case against that foundation thing as well. I mean, talk about lunacy. It's no charity: it's not in the public interest. That's what Arpad said. Can you imagine? Photographs of the soul?! I never heard such rubbish. The poor man was out of his mind. If there was any doubt before.... And she was egging him on every step of the way, the Plotnick woman. Arpad also said something about undue process, or some kind of influence, I'm not sure. Something about that woman's evil role. So you see we have a very strong case."

All this was very interesting, but it left me wondering: why had they come to see me? As if she was reading my mind, she informed me that the meeting was Arpad's idea, though *his* idea was a conference that would include him and Gideon and Lisbeth. Katerina had vetoed that decisively. "I said to him, we can speak to him without you and Lisbeth, we have mouths, you know; and he is after all *so* expensive, he charges for things like this by the hour, and I said to Cranshaw, we don't need him. We can report to him and to Lisbeth; so here we are."

"And?"

"You understand: if we win, and Arpad is *sure* we'll win, then your clients won't get a penny. Not a penny. We'll get it all. You know that."

"Not necessarily," I said. "*If* you win, and it's a big if, then the will goes down the tubes; but maybe there's an earlier will, and we'd have to look at that one then."

"Oh, but there isn't any earlier will."

"There isn't? How do you know?"

"Because we looked for one. His lawyer, that Gideon person, said he didn't know about any other wills. Not that I trust him. But after father died, Cranshaw and I, we had to take care of all the details.... We went to this funeral parlor, they wanted to sell us some sort of expensive coffin. Imagine! As if father would have wanted us to spend that kind of money. It's really disgusting, those places, they have coffins lined with some sort of upholstery, ridiculous, I mean, the man is dead, we're not worried about bedsores. No, we had him cremated.... We have the ashes... in a lovely urn, I keep it on the mantelpiece. And we went to the apartment. We had no key, of course, but the manager let us in, he didn't want to, said it wasn't allowed. But I insisted, we're his children. He gave us such a hard time, especially because of the police and all that crime scene nonsense. But I don't take no for an answer, and frankly, we had to bribe him, it was disgusting, but in the end, well, he had to do it."

"We thought there might be money there. Father had a lot of money," Cranshaw said.

She gave him a withering look of disdain. "Cranshaw, please," she said. "Don't be so crass. Yes, if there was money there lying around, we would have tried to keep that woman from getting it. She might have had a key to the place, for all we know. We wanted to protect his things, really. And well, just to see things. He was our father after all, and we hadn't been in the apartment for months, maybe years. And, yes, we were looking to see if there was a will, or any other documents...."

"And you didn't find a will, I assume," I said.

"You don't know what it was like, you can't imagine the filth. Newspapers from the year one, I swear. All yellow and disgusting. Really, I thought I'd be sick. Cranshaw too. There was this moldy smell. Honestly, I don't know how he could have lived there. I broke down and cried, I really did, thinking of my father in that place. I know, we had quarreled. He was bitter... but that was because of his mental state. I truly believe that. Deep down he must have loved us. We were his children."

Cranshaw nodded his head.

I asked: "Did you find anything of significance?"

"No… not so far. We were wondering about, well, possibly some sort of insurance policy, or a key to a safe deposit box, or stocks and bonds or valuables. But all we found was an insurance policy, years and years old, that he used to have. The money was supposed to go to his wife, but Mother died a long time ago, and he had canceled the policy. Oh, yes, and something that looked like a will, twenty years old, written on scratch paper; it left everything to mother, but it was all canceled and defaced with pen scratching. Nothing else."

"The album," Cranshaw said, in a low voice.

She looked at him fiercely. "It doesn't concern him, Cranshaw. Why bring it up? It's strictly personal."

"It meant a lot to me," he said. "I can't imagine where it's gone to."

"Cranshaw has this sentimental side," she said, turning to me. "He's referring to a photo album. Father had a photo album with all sorts of family pictures. Especially pictures of our dear mother."

"I wanted a picture of her. I don't have one," Cranshaw said in a lugubrious tone.

"We always loved to look at that album," she said to me. "And now, funny thing, it seems to be gone. I saw it there the last time I visited our father. He kept it on an old wooden desk he had. It isn't there now. Why would somebody steal it? When we saw it was missing, we wondered, what else is gone? Maybe this was a burglary after all. Maybe a burglar killed him."

"The police don't think so," I said.

"I know that," she said. "But I did think, at first, it has to be a burglar. The neighborhood he lived in! All those disgusting people, high on drugs, and homeless people on the street, pushing those grocery carts. I thought somebody must have broken in, some drug addict. I know the place was a pig sty, but there must have been people who knew, somehow, that father had all this money. They might have thought, he's a miser, he must keep it in the house, under a mattress or whatever. He didn't of course. Turned out, he had a lot of bank accounts. He must have loved going to the bank. But they wouldn't know that."

She went on: "I hope the police know what they're doing. Can you imagine, somebody coming in and killing father. Why? And why take the album, if that's what happened. Maybe father destroyed it in a fit of anger.... Or maybe somebody took it, took other things, to make it look like burglary, even though it wasn't. I just don't know."

I shrugged my shoulders.

"It's such an awful situation," she said. "It was so awful for me and for Cranshaw, when we were told he was dead. Then, later, when they told us that it was murder, I mean, that somebody killed our dear father deliberately, and they thought it wasn't a burglar, but cold-blooded murder. I tell you, I nearly fainted from shock. And Cranshaw, poor soul... and what makes it even more horrible was, when we talked about it, we thought, who could have done this terrible thing, and we came to the obvious conclusion! Who else?"

"Who do you mean?" I asked.

"Well, isn't it as plain as the nose on your face? That awful woman, Fern Plotnick! She did it for the money. Isn't that the usual reason?"

"But... your father put her in charge of his estate: what more would she want?"

She gave me a sharp, telling glance, as if to say, how naïve can you be. "Oh, yes, and she wanted that. But she was afraid he was going to change his mind, change his will, leave her out entirely. That's why she had to do something. That's why she had to get rid of him."

"Change his will? In what way? Did he say anything about changing his will?"

"Oh, he didn't say anything. Not to us, anyway. He wasn't on speaking terms with us. He acted as if we were dead. His own flesh and blood. I wrote him a letter, I reminded him of his duties, and I said, let's let bygones be bygones. Cranshaw and I, we wanted to be part of his family again. My heart was broken, believe me. But he never answered the letter.... This was not so long before he died. I'm sure *she* was there all the time, and she must have known what was going on in his poor mixed-up brain. After all, she was working on him constantly, poisoning his mind. He was going to change things. That awful man, Gideon, he knew about it."

"You spoke to Gideon Grambling?"

"Oh yes. He was father's lawyer. Yes, indeed. I called him. I even went to his office. I had to know what was going on. He didn't want to speak to me, but as I told you, I don't take no for an answer. Well, he was pretty close-mouthed. I did get hints, though he refused to give details, of course. And then father died before he could make any of those changes, whatever they might have been. Maybe he was going to relent and leave us some money. Not that we cared for the money, but *family*, oh dear yes, family. That's what counts."

Cranshaw nodded and Katerina wiped away a tear or two.

"It had to be that woman," she said, "that Plotnick woman. Who else could come in and out? Remember that: nobody broke in. That should tell you something. *We* didn't have a key."

I asked: "Did Fern Plotnick have a key?"

"Does it matter? She practically lived there. Maybe he let her in and then she killed him, just like that."

I'll spare you another long speech about the sheer awfulness of Fern Plotnick. I think Katerina would have gone on indefinitely, but I had another client coming in, and I had to suggest gently that perhaps it was time for them to go. Gentleness, however, had no effect; and finally, I had to insist on their leaving. I said I had to be in court. That wasn't true of course—I almost never go to court—but it's the one thing that seems to impress my clients, and is the best excuse I know for getting rid of them.

After they were gone, I saw my client, a man from India with a high-pitched voice who was some sort of tech person, and who wanted to set up a trust for his daughter. He was divorced and his ex-wife had custody. This was, I'm afraid, not one of those friendly divorces. The little girl was six years old. Rajiv insisted that I had to make sure the money could never, ever, under any circumstances, go to his ex-wife. "I don't want her to get a penny of it. Not a penny. She's already taken me to the cleaners." I took notes. "I worked for that money," he said, "I built up a business. What did she do? She played bridge all day long."

When he was gone, I sat back in my chair and thought about my visit from Katerina and Cranshaw. What did they have in mind? Why had they come? It was certainly an unconventional move. But they were, after all, unconventional people. Katerina, at least. I decided they wanted information, which in fact I had no power to give them. I was the lawyer for their enemies. And Katerina, clearly, was a woman who marched right in and took charge, a woman who, as she told me, "didn't take no for an answer." Or perhaps she wanted to plant in my mind the idea that Fern Plotnick was a ruthless killer.

Fern Plotnick? Cold-blooded murder? It seemed very unlikely. And if she had, in fact, killed Rupert Mobius, she would lose her position under the will. That would hardly do much good for Katerina and Cranshaw Mobius.

There was another possibility. Perhaps Katerina was simply reconnoitering. There were hints in the air about a settlement. Gideon was managing the estate of Rupert Mobius and he would be clearly involved in any settlement; but Derek and Doris would have a role, too, since they were heirs to half the estate of their great-uncle... and that would bring me into the picture.

It was hard to like Gideon Grambling: he was a vain

and arrogant man. That he had to deal first with the old skinflint, Mobius, and then with the likes of Katerina Mobius, not to mention Fern Plotnick, gave me a certain amount of guilty and malicious pleasure.

7

I didn't like Gideon, as I said. But we were entangled in the same sordid affair and I had to rely on his professional competence, after all.

Shortly after the visit from Katerina and Cranshaw, I called Gideon. Ms. Guthrie answered the phone. She was frosty and supercilious as usual. I wondered if she treated everyone that way or was the attitude mainly reserved for downmarket suburban lawyers, bill collectors, and telemarketing pests?

Once past this dragon guarding the castle, I was able to talk to Gideon. I told him all about the visit, and, as I expected, he was quite exasperated. Particularly about "the fools at the apartment building! They should have never let those two in. Especially her. She's quite impossible. And, after all, it's a crime scene: they have absolutely no business barging in. Absolutely none."

"Well, you've met Katerina," I said. "She can be quite persistent."

"And their interests are clearly adverse to the estate. They've filed a lawsuit against the estate. They are not to be trusted. That woman had the colossal gall to come here and harangue me. I had half a mind to call their attorney and insist that they stay away. And to think that they were allowed to rummage through the apartment! That was completely irregular. Completely. They could have taken away valuable documents! I'll make *sure* it doesn't happen again."

Gideon also suggested that I meet him at the apartment, perhaps with Derek or Doris or both, and that we should take a look for ourselves. I agreed, and we dickered for a while about setting a time. Afterwards, I called my clients, and told them about the arrangement, and asked if they wanted to come. Derek said he was too busy: I think this was a polite lie. I liked Derek, but I had the impression he was a bit lazy and spoiled. Doris, on the other hand, was more than willing to come. She said she had something to do in the city that day, anyway, and would meet me at the apartment.

I drove into the city on Highway 101. It was a clear, crisp day, very California. I live only half an hour away from San Francisco, but as I said, it's surprising how rarely I go there. As I entered the city with the Bay on my right, I was struck as usual by the rows of neat, pastel-colored houses, snaking up the sides of the hills. The tall buildings of downtown poked their heads into a few bunches of puffy white clouds.

Rupert's apartment building was in a dingy area south of Market Street. There were a few scraggly signs of gentrification: a Burmese restaurant, a small hotel that had obviously been renovated, and, a block away, a spanking new apartment building, shiny and bold, clearly betting on the future of the neighborhood. Still, in general, the area was ankle deep, so to speak, in the muck of urban decay. Rupert's building was particularly shabby. One side of the building faced a vacant lot, and looked somehow naked and ashamed. The front of the building was spattered with spray paint. Rupert had lived on the second floor up rickety stairs. Gideon was standing at the open door. He had a sour look on his face, like somebody sucking on a lemon. This was obviously not the sort of place where clients of Gideon's usually made their homes.

We had to wait for Doris, who was somewhat late, so we went into a kind of living room. I pushed a pile of papers to one side and sat down on a moth-eaten sofa. Gideon obviously preferred standing.

When Doris arrived, we got to work. It was a small apartment: a living room, one bedroom, and another small room that had no obvious use. This room was empty except for some wooden crates and boxes here and there on the floor, a broken chair, and a sort of wooden desk. Rupert must have used this room as a kind of study. There was also a tiny kitchen and an equally tiny bathroom with a tub. The place was deeply dispiriting. It had been a crime scene, and maybe the police, when they were done with what they had to do, tidied up a bit. If so, it hardly showed. There were piles of papers all over the bedroom, yellowing copies of the *Wall Street Journal* from years before, and other papers and magazines all heaped up higgledy-piggledy. In the bedroom was a single somewhat dilapidated bed, or rather a futon covering some sort of wooden framework.

Everything was dirty; everything was in terrible shape. He did have some kind of laptop computer, sitting on the desk in the small room. But since we had no idea what the password was, we couldn't find out if he had anything of interest in his files. Gideon said he would take care of this problem. I'm sure some computer geek—an extremely common species in Silicon Valley—would know how to crack the code.

We began to go through some of the drawers in the desk. There were all sorts of old bills, receipts, and papers. At first, we found very little of interest. One drawer was full of wires, coils, old paper clips, and broken pencils. Doris had brought with her some sort of hand sanitizer, and she sprayed some of it on her hands periodically. That struck me as a very good idea.

All this was grubby, dirty, and unrewarding work. We finished with the desk, and started on the drawers of the dresser in the bedroom. It was a substantial piece of furniture which might have seen better days, but in its present state looked as if it had been dragged in from Goodwill. The late Mr. Mobius was not the sort of man who folded his underwear neatly. Or folded his underwear at all. At least the socks, underwear, and shirts did look reasonably clean.

In the bottom drawer, we finally found something at least vaguely interesting. It was a kind of notebook, or datebook, for the current year. Mobius apparently never made regular entries: it certainly didn't qualify as a diary. And it was hard to read his spidery handwriting. Occasionally, he entered something that was more than perfunctory chiefly, I gathered, to vent his ample supply of spleen. One entry was about Katerina, who had apparently phoned that day: "My daughter the blood-sucker. The vampire. She wants my money." Another entry, about Cranshaw, was not much better. "She wraps him around her little finger. Is this a son of mine? No wonder his wife threw him out."

"Who was Cranshaw married to?" I asked Gideon.

"Some woman named Crystal Fox. It didn't last very long. No children, as I think I told you. She moved to Arizona."

I sat down on one of the few chairs in the living room, pushing some of the debris to one side, and continued leafing through the notebook. There were some strange entries about money, or, rather, *payments* of money. "Gave X another $3,000." No explanation of who X was, and why, in a private notebook, X was referred as X and not as Sam or Mary or Joe. Why was Rupert hiding the identity of X?

One entry was weird, to say the least. "Phone call. A message from the spirit world. Talked to Fern. She vouches for it. Selected people get these messages." And another one: "Fern says my nephew is trying to communicate with me. Fern says it is important. She says he is in the spirit world. She says I must listen carefully." And one more: "Another message. Fern says his soul is roaming, looking to enter our domain." And right after this, another brief and gnomic entry: "Stock market down 200 points. Call broker. Visit from the spirits."

As a member of the California bar, I take seriously

my ethical obligations. I would never destroy a document that had bearing on the affairs of my clients. But this notebook was very bad news for Derek and Doris. Obviously, Katerina and Cranshaw had never seen it. It would have supported their claim that the man was incompetent; that he lacked the mental equipment to make out a valid will. It was also evidence of the influence of Fern Plotnick. Not that she came off any better than Rupert did. If the will failed, Derek and Doris would lose everything. And so would I.

The entries became fairly sporadic in the month before Rupert Mobius died. Maybe he was busy, maybe he was sick. For the day he died, there was a short entry: "Simon coming. Have to break the news to him. Also Mr. Big." I wondered, of course, what this meant. What was the news he had to "break" to his brother? And who was Mr. Big?

I was going to find out the answer, as it happens; but not right away.

I showed the notebook to Gideon and Doris. I said to Doris, "This isn't good for us, Doris. It feeds the argument that the man was deranged, and that hurts our cause."

"Can't we just get rid of it?" she said.

"No," I said.

"Do we have to show it to them at all?"

"I think so," I said. "Gideon, what do you think?" I tried to hand him the notebook. He took it gingerly, holding it by the upper right corner, as if it was unclean and contagious. He leafed through it and I showed him some of the choice passages. Gideon was not the sort of man who commits himself on issues of law. When he put the notebook down, he reminded me (as if I needed reminding) that courts really hate to strike down wills, even when the testator was "quite eccentric, and even delusional."

"He had his odd ways," Gideon added. "I grant you that. And this, uh, document certainly points in that direction. But in the end, the evidence is, shall we say, quite ambivalent. Look at this: market down 200 points. Broker calls. That's not the behavior of someone who's incompetent to make out a will. I think we have a better case than one might think."

"I hope so," I said.

We found nothing more of any particular interest or relevance. Oh yes, there was a dead mouse in the kitchen. Very dead, the way dead mice look, with its mouth open and its disgusting little teeth plainly showing. I saw it first, and managed to keep it from Doris. I picked it up by its tail, and put it into a wastebasket.

Then we all went home. I can't answer for Doris or Gideon, but I felt depressed. The fog had rolled in, making the city look gloomy and disheartened, and that only added to my mood.

8

I'm sure Doris gave her brother a full report about our adventures, but I felt I had a duty to do this as well. I called him in the evening.

He said, yes, he had heard it all from Doris. Then he added: "I... I've been meaning to call you, Frank. I really have to talk to you."

"Sure thing, Derek. What about?"

"I don't want to say anything on the phone...."

It seemed quite mysterious and I thought I detected a bit of agitation or nervousness in his voice. We made an arrangement to meet at my office the following day.

Derek came exactly on time and sat down across from me. He was somewhat distraught: his face was pale, he avoided eye contact, and he fidgeted endlessly in the chair. "I have something I have to tell you," he said.

"Sure."

"I know you'll keep it confidential. Lawyers have to, don't they?"

"They do. Absolutely. You can trust me."

"I took this course in legal ethics in law school," he said. "God, it was boring. All those rules! But I do remember the part about confidentiality. That's still the rule, Frank, isn't it?"

"Positively."

"Anyway, there's nobody else I can talk to. It's been... very hard for me," he said. I said nothing, waiting for him to go on. "It's not an easy thing to say."

"Derek, for God's sake, out with it. What's bothering you?"

"You know this business about... Uncle Rupert. He was murdered, OK, we talked about that. I told you they suspected my grampa, and... there was an investigation, and all that, the police, detectives, reporters too, calling on the phone. I guess they couldn't really find any real proof, anything that could stick. I don't know what they were doing, maybe they had something going; but anyway, he wasn't arrested or anything like that. And then he died, and that was the end of it, as far as I know."

"Right, Derek," I said.

"Well, about a week before he died, Grampa knew that he was very sick, heart failure. He had it for years, but it was getting worse, maybe the doctor said something, you know, that he didn't have long to live. Anyway, he called me on the phone—he didn't do that very often—he said, Derek, I want you to come see me, I have something important to tell you. So naturally I went, and he was sitting up in bed, looking very sick, there was even a nurse there, but he chased her out of the room. So then he said to me, Derek, this is a tough thing for me, but I don't want to die with something on my conscience. I want to tell you the truth. OK, I said. Then he said to me, Derek, I was the one who killed my brother Rupert."

"He said that?"

"He said it. Just like that. As you can imagine, it was a terrific shock. Not that the thought hadn't crossed my mind, how could it not? I mean, he was just about the last person, or maybe *the* last, to see Uncle Rupert alive. But I didn't believe he actually *did* it! I mean, he was old, and very sick and all that. Then he said it again. Derek, it was me. I was the one. And he said, I've written it all out, a full confession. He handed me an envelope, a sealed envelope, and he said, this is the story. If something happens to me--I'm an old man, I haven't long to live--I want you to give this to the police."

"But you didn't," I said.

"I didn't. Right. But this was because he said to me, Derek, you don't have to do this right away. I'll be dead soon. I said, no Grampa, don't say that, but he brushed this aside. He said the police think I did it. Maybe they're going to arrest me, but at my age, who cares? I'm too sick to stand trial, and they know that."

"So why confess?" I asked. "Was it his conscience or something like that?"

Derek said, "Maybe. I don't know. He said, though, I wanted this down in black and white in case something happens to me."

"In case something happened? That sounds funny. Do you think he was afraid of something? Or worried?"

"Well, I don't know. Maybe. He did seem on edge. I thought at first, maybe he knows who killed Uncle Rupert, and maybe he's afraid for himself. But that wasn't it. He said, if the police try to pin this on somebody, you know, he said, the police do that sort of thing, just to pretend they've solved the crime, they plant evidence, and he went on and on with this stuff about the police, and the point was, he said, don't let them screw some innocent man. He said, promise me, Derek. If that happens, you'll give this to the police. And I said, I promise. So here I am. I've got the envelope, but I haven't done anything with it."

"A sealed envelope? You haven't read it?"

"Well, actually I have. I steamed it open, and I read it, and then I closed it up again, and put scotch tape on it."

"And it was a confession?"

"It was."

"He killed his own brother?"

"I'm telling you what he said."

"Did he say why?"

"Well," Derek said, "he did. Sort of. In the letter. He said it was all about money. He went to see Rupert, he said, and Rupert told him he was going to change his will. He wasn't going to leave anything at all to the family. He said, you people don't need the money. He was going to leave the whole thing to this Plotnick woman and this crazy trust."

"Was he actually going to do that?"

"Well, it's what my grandfather told me. And in this letter here, Grampa went on and on about how he did it, and all for the sake of the family, etc. He went to see his brother, and he learned this thing about the will, and this Plotnick woman, and the damn foundation. He said to Rupert, the whole thing is nuts, if you ask me, and Rupert said, well, I'm not asking you. And they got into a terrific argument."

"And that's when... when it happened?"

"I guess. I can imagine how mad Grampa was. All those millions and millions of dollars, and that crazy foundation, and the crazy woman; and we were going to be cut out totally. Him and me and Doris. Grampa wrote that he tried to talk Rupert out of it, and then they were screaming at each other. And he felt, well, desperate. He was a sick old man, he didn't want the money, but he wanted it for his family. For his grandchildren. Actually, he said something peculiar: for his grandchildren, past and future."

"Past and future?"

"Those were the words. Past and future. I mean, obviously, there aren't going to be any more grandchildren. I think he must have meant, great-grandchildren; me and Doris, after all, we're young, we'll have kids someday, I hope. Anyway, they were arguing, and Grampa made up his mind to kill him before he could do this. And he says he knew it was the wrong thing to do, but he did it anyway, and he's sorry now, truly sorry, and so on."

"Are you sure he wrote this?"

"Well, it's in his handwriting. I'm sure of that."

There was something fishy about the whole story. Murder is a pretty extreme thing to do. I know, people do kill for money. But still, it didn't seem likely in this situation. According to what Derek himself had told me, the old man wasn't that close to his grandchildren. He certainly didn't sound like such a devoted grandfather, so warm a family man, that he would kill his own brother to save money for Derek and Doris. They weren't exactly on welfare to begin with.

Still, *somebody* killed the old man. The police had always suspected Simon Mobius. They didn't have any other suspects as far as I knew. And, to be sure, even though the grandchildren didn't *need* the money, there were millions and millions of dollars at stake: a share in the Mobius estate would be a lot of money, even for people who are fairly well off.

But to kill his own brother? I kept coming back to that point. I had never met either of the Mobius brothers. For all I knew, they were homicidal lunatics. But statistics were against this idea. Old people do not kill other people. It doesn't take much strength to pull a trigger, but still, murder is a young man's game. Almost always.

Even if you accepted Simon's confession at face value, there was something about it that nagged at me. Was the old man worried about something? Was he afraid of something or someone? What led him to write all this down?

There was something else I had to ask Derek: "Did your grandfather have a gun? They never found the murder weapon."

"I have no idea. I wouldn't have thought he was the gun type, but who knows? Maybe he was a member of the NRA. I wouldn't put it past him. Anyway, the police can trace things, can't they? And don't you have to register them or something?"

"I honestly don't know. But even if you're supposed to register," I said, "that doesn't mean that people will actually do that, I mean, register. Anyway, did anybody find a gun?"

"No," he said. "As far as I know, the police never said

anything about a gun. But does it matter? Somebody shot him. And it's easy to get rid of a gun, isn't it? Just toss it in the bay or throw it in a dumpster. You wouldn't expect the guy who shot Uncle Rupert to just leave the gun lying around."

Yes, it was easy to throw a gun into the bay or a dumpster. But the whole story smelled bad. Simon Mobius was a weak old man: he wasn't even driving any more, if I remembered correctly. I had to assume the "confession" was genuine, that is, in the sense that it wasn't a forgery. But was Simon telling the truth? For that matter, was Derek telling the truth? In both cases, I had my doubts.

Meanwhile, I had done some research into one of the vexing legal questions dogging the estate. If in fact the old man had killed his brother, it wasn't clear to me under California law whether Derek and Doris could receive their share of the estate. I thought, on the whole that they would. But I wasn't sure.

On the other hand, the idea that the old man killed his brother was just an idea. No proof. No arrest, no trial, and old Simon was conveniently dead. In that case, what happens? In that case, I suppose that Derek and Doris were rightful heirs. But the document, the confession, that was a real complication. I shuddered to think of the consequences if it got into the hands of the police. But was it ethical to suppress it? Derek was my client, and anything he told me was strictly confidential. Still....

I called Gideon. First I had to deal at some length with Ms. Guthrie, who behaved as if she was secretary to the head of the United Nations, or to the Pope, and whose main duty was to keep people from talking to her boss.

"May I ask in what connection is this call?" she said

in her most haughty voice.

I can't imagine that she took that tone with clients. I had the feeling she recognized my voice, and that in her books I was a small-town, small-potatoes lawyer.

Eventually I got through to Gideon after being told he was "in conference," hanging up, and calling back. He was brusque on the phone; I told him that I had to be in the city the next day on business, and could I have fifteen minutes or so of his time? We made an arrangement, and I appeared, exactly on time, at his office. It was eleven in the morning. Ms. Guthrie gave me a cold look when I entered. I sat in an easy chair, waiting for Gideon to be free. ("He's on a conference call," she said.) I sat by a small end table piled high with appropriate magazines, no doubt for the edification of his clients as they waited for the great lawyer to be free. I leafed through the pages of *Forbes*, which had a listing of people who had more than a billion dollars, and I daydreamed about life with a billion dollars. I was drifting off the coast of Fiji under the tropical sun, when I was summoned at last.

"Gideon," I said, after he waved me into a leather chair in his office, "I have to ask you a question. Did you have conversations with Mobius before he died, about changing his will?"

"I'm glad you said 'before he died'; if I listened to Ms. Plotnick, I might very well be getting messages about the will *after* he died."

I hadn't attributed to Gideon a rich sense of humor. Or any sense of humor. Or was it humor? He, after all, did have the unenviable task of dealing with Fern Plotnick.

I chuckled and repeated my question. "Was the old man thinking of changing his will?"

"Why are you posing this particular question?" he said. "I showed you the text of his will. Whether he would have wanted to alter it at some point is really quite irrelevant, don't you agree?"

"I believe he went to see you the day before he died."

"I really don't think I need to comment on that. I don't see how you can know that."

"It was in his diary, Gideon. Datebook, whatever you want to call it. You saw that yourself."

"And so?"

"So we know he wanted to see you. Did he actually come?"

He hesitated a second. "May I ask why you want to know this? As I said, it is legally quite irrelevant, whether we discussed any changes or not. The man is dead. No changes were made."

"Please Gideon, indulge me. Did he or didn't he come here and discuss changes to his will?"

Another hesitation. Then he said. "All right. Yes, we did discuss the possibility of... well, let's say we discussed legal matters."

"Gideon, why are you so vague?" I said. "Of course you discussed legal matters. You wouldn't talk about the weather or the war in Afghanistan. You were his lawyer, for God's sake. *Was it about his will?*"

"Really, Frank...."

"Was it or wasn't it about his will?"

"I prefer to keep these matters confidential," he said. "My ethical obligations...."

"Gideon," I said, "the man is dead. Murdered, in fact. I took the bar a long time ago, and I don't exactly keep up with legal ethics, but I do think you could help me out here."

He became a bit testy: "I don't recall that anybody deputized you as, uh, a detective here. I can't quite see the relevance of your question."

"Can I spell it out for you? The interests of my clients—and yours, I might add—might depend on this damn murder thing. I haven't been reading Scott Turow or Sue Grafton recently, but isn't it the case that motive is pretty important, if you're trying to unravel a mystery? Now, then, if the old man was thinking of changing his will, that would have an impact, wouldn't it?"

In the end, Gideon reluctantly agreed. Personally, I think he had always seen the point. He simply was unwilling to admit me as a partner, so to speak, in this tawdry affair. And yes, it was true: the old man was thinking of changing his will.

"He told me so. In broad outline. We didn't get down to the details. It was a preliminary discussion. He wanted to increase the share of his foundation, that much I know. Whether he intended to eliminate his family's share, I'm not sure. Perhaps. I had an urgent appointment, I had a client coming in, a very very rich individual, one of my best clients, a venture capitalist, and I couldn't waste time. Besides, well, frankly, I was irritated. He showed up without an appointment, and was sitting in my outer office. I have *very particular* clients, wealthy people, people who *matter* in society, and Mobius was sitting there looking like something the cat dragged in. I mean, his behavior, as usual, was intolerable. Ms. Guthrie was scandalized. I had to break off the conversation before, well, my client was due. I said to him, look Mobius, can't this wait a day or so? Why don't you make an appointment? Of course he was annoyed. He was the most difficult person. But he had to agree and so we made an arrangement for the next day. Little did I know that the next day he would be dead...."

Once Gideon began to open up, he told me, in addition to what I wanted to know about the will, many other things as well. Gideon, somehow, had quite a bit of inside information about the progress of the police investigation of the Mobius murder. He had "influential friends, people in the know," he said proudly, and his "connections" apparently included the police department. At least he hinted as much.

I gathered that the death of Rupert Mobius was more or less a cold case. This was probably because the police assumed Simon Mobius had killed his brother, and Simon was conveniently dead. I asked Gideon about the murder weapon, and he said that no gun had ever been registered to either Rupert or Simon Mobius. Of course, that really didn't prove anything. There are all sorts of ways to get guns, he told me.

I personally do not have a gun and do not want a gun. I have no sympathy for the NRA, to be honest: some of those gun people seem like lunatics. Would Thomas Jefferson and his buddies, if they came back to life, really want people to own Uzis, or submachine guns, or bazookas? Especially if they discovered how many crazy people there are roaming about in the United States of America?

The gun people are always talking about constitutional rights, but the second amendment seems to be the only one they care about.

I never met either Rupert or Simon Mobius. Maybe cranky old men like guns. You can never tell.

On my way out, I decided to ask Ms. Guthrie a question or two. She was even more reluctant than Gideon, but I managed eventually to pierce her steely reserve. I think what did the trick were dark comments about how serious it was to withhold information, seeing as this was a murder case. And I tried to insinuate—a little white lie— that an active investigation was ongoing, and in fact was on the brink of heating up.

"I don't see why that matters. I have no information," she said, "and therefore I have nothing to withhold."

"Mr. Mobius was here the day before he died," I said. "That would be very interesting. For the police, I mean."

"Oh, but he wasn't here. That awful man. You know, Mr. Grambling didn't like to have that man around. He tried to keep him from coming. He said to me, Ms. Guthrie, tomorrow Ms. Murgatroyd is coming for a very important session. Ms. Murgatroyd, as you know, is a very important woman, a woman of substance. She inherited a fortune from her father, the railroad and real estate man. She's quite particular. Lord knows what she'd think if she saw somebody who looked like Mobius. So Mr. Grambling said to me, call Mobius, and ask him if we can put this meeting off. Make it some other day. Don't let him come in the same day as Ms. Murgatroyd."

"But he did come."

"No, he didn't. I called him, and told him we wanted to delay the meeting, and he said, your boss, Mr. High and Mighty, he doesn't fool me. I wasn't born yesterday. I can read his mind. He doesn't want me around. He wants my money and my business, but he doesn't want me. All right. Tell him to come here."

"And you said?"

"I said: Mr. Grambling doesn't make house calls. And he was so rude and indignant, honestly. His tone of voice.... He said, well, tell him to make an exception, or I'm through with him. I'll go to some other lawyer. Have him come here at five o'clock, or something like that. I don't remember the exact words."

"And did he go? Mr. Grambling, I mean. Did he... make the house call, as you put it?"

"I wouldn't think so. I have no idea. That day, Mr. Grambling left the office at four: he said he had some urgent business."

"And that was the day Rupert Mobius died."

"Really, I don't know that. I'd have to check the files."

I smiled at her and left. But it left me wondering: did Gideon Grambling swallow his pride, did he in fact go to see Rupert Mobius in his wretched apartment? But that would put him on the scene the very day Rupert died, maybe the very hour and minute. I was itching to find out whether this was the case. Could I ask Gideon whether he had gone to the house? All the way home I kept asking myself that question. No obvious answer came to mind. One thing was clear though: Gideon had lied to me. A bold-faced lie.

I had the feeling that almost everyone who spoke to me was lying about one thing or another. But there was nothing much I could do about this.

9

The next few days were uneventful. Meaning, life went on. Celia and I went to the movies; we had dinner with neighbors; my daughters quarreled with each other and with us. The usual story. And I was quite busy at work.

Surprisingly, I had a call from Doris Mobius, who wanted to see me. "You and Derek, I assume?"

"No. I want to see you myself. No Derek this time."

She came the next day. As I have said, she was an attractive woman in her late 20's. I realized I had paid little attention to her before. This is probably the inborn sexism that's common to all of us males. I had looked on her as a kind of appendage to Derek. Or perhaps I wasn't being fair to myself. Derek, after all, was the primary client. He was the one who came to see me. But Doris was also a client, insofar as she was a beneficiary of her grandfather's estate.

"Let me begin," she said, "by telling you a little something about myself. I had, well, a kind of tough adolescence. Derek was a good boy, more or less. Oh, there were problems, but boys are expected to be a little wild, and everybody forgives them. But I was a disappointment to my mother and my grandmother. I won't go into details. I've always had an adventurous streak in me. I went backpacking in Europe with a friend, when I was 16. The friend was a guy. My mother freaked."

I can imagine. My older daughter is 16. Is this what was coming for me? Off to Europe with some pimply creep, carrying a knapsack, sharing a sleeping bag, having sex in a series of youth hostels and grubby hotels, all over Belgium and France? God forbid.

"I love to travel," she said. "I've always had a travel bug. Did Derek tell you about my trip to Australia? I suppose he did, but not the whole story. Yes, I went to Australia. I went with a friend of mine. A guy, but a different guy. I'm not 16 anymore. It doesn't matter what guy. We broke up halfway through, and he went on to Bali. Good riddance. A real jerk, but that's water under the bridge. It was a vacation, basically, but I had an ulterior motive. Ever since I was a kid, I felt a loss... I missed having a father. Not that I don't appreciate all that my mother's done for us. Anyway, now I do, but I didn't always. Derek, he never cared, about the missing father. But I did. I wanted to find him."

"You didn't, though," I said.

"Well, basically, that's true. I didn't find him. Piers Mobius, wow, that was one elusive guy. I think that's the only way to describe it. Elusive. Like, he left traces everywhere, if you know what I mean. People, things. But I never caught up with him, and nobody knew exactly where he was. I talked to a lot of people. Practically everything I heard was negative, I tell you, it was downright depressing. This man was my father! And what I found out, he was a real sociopath, maybe even violent. And I guess he was trying to make himself scarce, I don't know. I'm pretty sure he was the sort of man who wouldn't care at all that his daughter was in Australia looking for him. Oh yes, one more thing. When the boat sank, the one he was on, my friends in Australia, they told me, there were all sorts of rumors. About somebody maybe sabotaging the boat; I mean, yes, for sure there was a storm, but really, what happened to the boat, maybe it wasn't an accident. Or not a pure accident."

"So, the rumor was that somebody killed him?"

"I know what you're thinking. It runs in the family, isn't that what's on your mind? He killed somebody, maybe; and then somebody killed him; and then his father, the old man, kills his brother: is that what you're thinking?"

"God no, Doris," I said. "Really, I wasn't thinking about that. Honest to God."

"Anyway," she said, "I heard from my friends in Australia once in a while; and they told me nobody had any real proof or anything, and of course, the boat and the body are at the bottom of the Pacific Ocean somewhere. So it's just talk. But the reason why there was so much talk, well, was because he had so many enemies."

"Enemies? What kind of enemies?"

"People he had cheated. And then there were all those women he was involved with. When I got there, people told me about one woman in particular, her name was Wanda. They were together, and she was a real piece of work. That was his girlfriend at the time."

"And did you meet this Wanda?"

"No, never. I lost their trail in Brisbane. He had been there with her, but now they were gone. Anyway, about that time, I was having my own troubles. Me and Justin, that's the guy I was with, well, it ended badly, but it wasn't a total loss. We had some good times. We spent a week on one of those little islands, on the Barrier Reef, that was really something. Snorkeling, that sort of thing. All the birds and fish: it was a beautiful place. And the weather was great. We had a great time, there. I wasn't even thinking about Piers Mobius at that point. But then, Justin started acting out, or—well, never mind. Long story short, I traveled a bit on my own, and then I came home. But I made some friends in Australia, and I'm still in contact with them. They're the ones that told me all about my father's accident."

"They never found the boat or the body?"

"No. The Pacific is a big ocean. Not that I think anybody spent millions looking for him, or his boat. I don't think many people shed tears over him. Not even Wanda, the girlfriend. The latest girlfriend. By the way, my friends just told me, they heard she was in the United States. With another boyfriend, somebody new."

Wanda and her boyfriends didn't interest me, not at that time. As far as I was concerned, she was a bit player in the drama. Later... but you'll see that shortly.

We talked estate business for a while. She was worried—no surprise—about the idea that her grandfather had killed his own brother. "If he had," she asked, "would that cost us our inheritance?" I had meant to do more research on this question, so I hedged. And I asked her, "Do you honestly think he could have done such a thing?"

"I don't know what to think. He was there that day. We know that. Still, he wasn't alone."

"He wasn't alone?"

"Grampa didn't drive any more. Not for the last six months at least. His eyesight was not so good, and he had been in a couple of accidents. It could have been worse: he crashed into this truck in a parking lot, you've seen the sort of thing: it was selling Mexican food. The construction workers buy stuff there. And here comes Grampa, and somehow he loses control, and there's tacos and tamales flying all over the place. A miracle nobody was hurt. They took his license away. Good thing, too."

"So... he took public transportation?"

"Well, sometimes," she said. "He used to take a train to the city, to see his brother; but that was getting harder, too, and he had to take a cab to the train station, you know, the Caltrain station. But Grampa hated to use a cab, he was from the old school, cabs were for rich people, he said. Anyway, Derek drove him...."

"Derek?"

"Of course. Who else? Didn't he tell you? I'm surprised. Yes, it was Derek who drove him to the city. Derek says he never went in the place. He just parked the car and sat there, listening to the radio. But I don't know if I believe him. How do we know that Derek didn't go up with Grampa?"

What was she hinting at? I asked her what that would mean, that is, that Derek was there?

"Oh, I know what you're thinking," she said. "You're thinking: what is this awful woman saying? Is she suggesting something terrible, something about her own brother? I'm not really saying anything. I'm just... well, just telling the truth. Derek drove Grampa to the city. That's the plain honest truth. I'm just saying this to you to keep the record straight. I haven't discussed this with Derek, or with Mother, or with anybody."

"But you must have some reason to talk to me about it. I know what you're saying, that you just want me to know, and you aren't doing anything but telling me the truth, the facts. But is that all, Doris? Is there something else?"

She looked unhappy, conflicted. She was quiet for a minute or two, and then she said: "I don't know what I'm trying to say, I really don't. Except for what I told you. It's been on my mind. It's bothering me. Look: I know what Grampa was like. The man was old, sick, feeble. Could hardly see, couldn't drive any more. He had congestive heart failure and a million other things. I can't imagine him actually killing somebody. It just doesn't make sense.... That's all. I'm not accusing Derek. Maybe it was somebody else. A bushy-haired stranger, a guy with one arm, like in that movie I saw. I'm just surprised Derek never talked about this."

Did she know about her grandfather's confession? Had Derek confided in her? I wished I knew. What was clear was that Derek hadn't told me the truth, the whole truth, and nothing but the truth. He never mentioned that he drove his grandfather. Never mentioned that he had been in the city at all. Why not? What was he hiding?

10

I had to get to Derek, and ask him about the events of that day. As luck would have it, he was coming by to talk about estate matters, how to pay the last phone and gas bills, and what to do about a small bank account his grandfather had. We talked about these things for a while, and then I asked him, point-blank, whether it was true that he drove his grandfather to his great-uncle's house the day Rupert Mobius died.

"Well, as I matter of fact I did. Grampa didn't drive anymore, and he didn't like public transportation."

"You never told me this," I said. I tried not to sound too harsh. Derek was a client, after all.

"Well, I didn't think it mattered," he said. Of course that was a lie, but I let it drop.

"I need to get this straight, Derek," I said. "You went upstairs with your grandfather...."

"Correction," he said. "I did not go upstairs. Yes, I did drive Grampa there. But I never went into the house. Would you? The place was disgusting. No, I found a parking space out front, which was something of a miracle in San Francisco, and I just sat in the car and fed the meter every half hour or so. I was reading a magazine. Grampa said, well this might take a while. I said, that's OK, I have no place to go."

"Did you see anybody else go in and out?"

"Hey, Frank, why are you asking these questions? Is it really any of your business?"

"OK, OK, don't get annoyed. I suppose it isn't any of my business. Maybe I was just curious. *Did* you see anybody else, though, I mean, coming in and out of the place?"

"I wasn't paying attention. Anyway, it's an apartment building. Lots of people live in it, if you can call that living. Maybe some people came and went, I wouldn't know."

"Did you see anything odd, did anything strike you as, well, out of the ordinary?"

"Really, Frank, what's the point of all this?" he said.

I had to tread carefully. "Maybe there isn't a point, Derek. I don't mean to pry. But it's not totally irrelevant, is it? I mean, to the question of who killed your uncle."

"No; but Frank, are you a detective? I don't think so. It's up to the police, isn't it? Anyway, I told you, my grandfather confessed. He said he did it. What more do you need?"

"Nothing, I guess. Especially if the police aren't interested in the case anymore. But if they suddenly decided to open the case again...."

"Why would they do that?"

"Well, because of Katerina and Cranshaw, maybe. If they think it would help their case, you know, accusing your grandfather, let's say, and then trying to cut you guys out of the estate somehow.... Could anybody back up your story?"

"What story?"

"Well, that you were sitting there, in the car...."

"No, of course not. I mean, people walked by, but that's nothing. I can't prove I was there. Well, wait: maybe. There was a black Mercedes parked just in front of me. I noticed it because, well, it's not exactly a Mercedes neighborhood, if you know what I mean. There was a guy sitting in the car, just sitting there. I couldn't see him really, just his back, and the fact that he was sitting there in the passenger seat. I couldn't quite see the driver, but I had the impression it was a woman. I think they could see me in the rear-view mirror. I noticed him, because I was wondering, who is this guy, and why is he sitting there? Why is the car there in the first place?"

"And then?"

"They drove away. That's all. Not much to go on, is it?"

"Do you know the license number?"

"Frank: get real. Of course not. Maybe people in books write down license numbers, but I don't. But listen, Frank: am I in trouble?"

"I don't think so. But if Katerina and Cranshaw do make a fuss... at that point, maybe you'll need a lawyer. I mean, I'm a lawyer, but not that kind of lawyer."

"Why would I need a lawyer? Why me?"

"Well, because.... Look, suppose they find out, your grandfather didn't drive any more, and they start wondering, well, how did he get to the city.... You see my point. They might want to ask you some questions."

Derek nodded. He still looked worried. He was silent for a few minutes, and then he said. "Frank, I haven't told you everything."

"You haven't? OK. What's the everything you haven't told me?"

"I was sitting there waiting Like I told you. Then my grandfather came down out of the building. He looked... funny."

"Funny?"

"Bothered. Worried. I can't describe it exactly. He was agitated about something. He said, we got to go. Now! Start the car. I'll tell you where to go. And he had a bag with him, an ordinary paper bag."

"A paper bag? Big or small?"

"Medium size. Look, I didn't measure it. Anyway, the bag was closed, it had Scotch tape around it. I said, what's in the bag, Grampa? He said, never mind. Just drive. I said, where am I driving to? He said, drive somewhere

where we can dump this bag in the bay or in the ocean, I don't care. One of the two. I said, are you going to tell me what's in the bag, or what this is all about?"

"Did he answer you?"

"He said I'm not going to tell you. And that was that. But then he wanted to know where I thought we could go, where it would be safe to drop it in the ocean, where nobody would find it. I knew a place, on the ocean side of the city, pretty deserted usually. There's a kind of cliff overlooking the water, and you can walk pretty much to the edge, and I thought that would be just the place, so I mentioned it to my grandfather. He said, sounds OK. Well, we drove there, near there anyway, and I parked the car, and he told me, now you do it, I can't go out there myself, I'm too damn old and feeble. And I want you to swear to me, on the Holy Bible or your mother's honor or whatever the hell you want to swear on, that you're not going to look inside the bag."

"And you did what he said?"

"I did. I walked out to the end of that cliff. There was nobody much around, and I leaned over the railing; and when I thought nobody was looking, I threw the bag as far as I could into the water. And that was that."

"Be honest with me, Derek: what do you think was inside the bag?"

"I think it was a gun, the one Grampa used to kill his brother. Don't think I haven't thought about this over and over again. Like, should I tell the police? But I was scared. Does this make me an accomplice or something? I mean, I never looked inside the bag. But it's only my say-so. The police, they can get mean, can't they?"

"I suppose they can, Derek. But let's not worry about it. Not now, anyway. Let's hope that the police just let things lie. I know Katerina and Cranshaw are going to try something, but maybe the police will ignore them. It's not like there's nothing else to investigate in San Francisco. So I wouldn't lose any sleep over this."

"I hope you're right," Derek said, on his way out the door.

11

After Derek left, I sat in my office thinking. I should have been working on other things, but I couldn't. I was intrigued by the black Mercedes. Of course, most likely it had nothing to do with the case. The car could be anything or anybody. It could have nothing to do with that particular apartment building. Parking spaces are a rare commodity, and maybe the black Mercedes had business two blocks away, and this was the only available parking spot.

But an idea kept popping into my head, a crazy idea: could that car belong, perhaps, to Gideon Grambling? I had no idea what kind of a car he drove, but he was just the type to own a black Mercedes.

Gideon didn't make "house calls." But he also did not want the old man in his office. And the datebook had mentioned that a visit was scheduled from "Mr. Big." That could be a sarcastic reference to Gideon.

But wasn't this nonsense? A man sitting in a car in the passenger seat. Was I really thinking: Gideon Grambling, fancy San Francisco lawyer, goes into this seedy apartment building, goes upstairs, kills his client to prevent him from changing his will, for whatever reason, then goes downstairs and sits in his car for half an hour? Does that make any sense? No, it doesn't. And who was the other person in the car? All sorts of weird ideas flashed through my mind. Gideon had hired a hit man, and that was the driver.

I know nothing about the habits of hit men. Are there even such things in real life, or is it only in the movies? How do you find one, anyway? Do they advertise on Craigslist?

Anyway, why would a hit man sit in the car for half an hour? And wouldn't Gideon want to be far, far away when the hit man struck?

I did feel it might pay to talk to Gideon.

I called him on the phone. Of course I didn't get him. Eventually, yes; but I'll spare you the long process of our phone tag.

"Frank, what can I do for you?" he said, in his oiliest voice, when I finally reached the great man.

"Gideon: the day your client died, didn't you drive over to his place?

A pregnant pause. "Why are you asking this question?"

I took a wild stab. "Or somebody drove you. You own a black Mercedes; and somebody saw the car, parked outside the building where Mobius lived. And I know he wanted you to come by and talk to him about his will."

I could tell, even on the phone, that Gideon's whole manner had just frozen over, like a pond in Moscow in winter. He said, "What is this all about, Frank? I fail to see how it's any of your business. Where I go and what I do is my own affair and nobody else's."

"You're absolutely right," I said. "I'm not prying" (a lie); "I just wanted to keep you abreast of things. I'm just letting you know that somebody saw your car."

"Did they? And how did they know it was mine?"

"I'd rather not answer that."

"Oh, come on, Frank. I don't know what game you're playing, but I think I have a right to tell you not to persist in this ridiculous cross-examination."

"Gideon," I said, "I'm not cross-examining you. I'm not trying to be hostile, anything like that. I'm just bringing you up to date, that's all."

"And this other person in this alleged car," he said. "Who is that supposed to be? Did your informant tell you?"

"Frankly, the driver wasn't visible...."

"Frank, what are you up to? I don't like any of this. What you're implying.... Remember, the case is closed. The murder case. Shut. Filed away."

"*Was* closed," I said. "Katerina and Cranshaw want it reopened."

He could have called my bluff. But instead he changed his tone—I suppose it was hearing the magic names of Katerina and Cranshaw who were, after all, threatening the estate which he wanted to manage (and which he wanted to milk for his fees). I could hear him sighing. Then he said: "Yes, it was my car. And yes, somebody drove me to the apartment. I... had had my eyes tested, went to the optometrist, so I didn't want to drive myself. Eyes dilated. Yes, we drove there. Is that a crime? I was profoundly irritated, and I finally said to myself, why am I doing this? My dignity, my reputation mean a lot to me, my position in the bar association.... I've been active for years in the city and there's talk that I might become head of the ethics committee. I'm proud of my position in society. Well, never mind all that. I was sitting in my car. I thought to myself, this man is rich. Yes, he's a client, but he's totally intolerable. He had threatened to go to another lawyer: he wanted me to come begging. I made up my mind then and there: no more. I would not go up to his disgusting apartment. If he went to another lawyer, so be it. Yes, I would lose money, but even that wasn't clear. He was the sort of client who haggles and bargains, as if professional services were something out of an eastern bazaar. I've already had a taste of that from him. I refuse to tolerate that. I am an attorney, a specialist, an expert. And I charge accordingly...."

"OK, OK, Gideon, I believe you. I was just curious.... Well, as you know, the man was murdered. Did you see anything, did you see anybody go in or out of the building?"

"I wasn't looking, Frank. I suppose people did go in and out. It's an apartment building, after all. I was absorbed in my own thoughts."

"You didn't see an elderly man carrying a paper bag?"

"No, I did not. An elderly man with a paper bag? What is *this* about?"

"It's about Rupert's brother, Simon Mobius. He was the last person to see his brother alive."

"Somebody saw him come out of the building, with a paper bag? My God, Frank, who were these busybodies who were observing all the goings-on at that building? I find this totally astonishing."

"I'd rather not say," I said, feebly. "But Simon Mobius *was* there, and he did come out of the building...."

"Of course he came out of the building. So what? And what was in this paper bag?"

"I don't know," I said. "Nobody saw what was in it."

"Well, if he was anything like his brother, it could have been leftovers from lunch or soda bottles he picked up out of the garbage."

"And," I went on, "it does seem as if Simon was the last person to see his brother alive."

"I imagine he was," Gideon said. "And the first person to see him dead, since it's more likely than not that Simon, shall we say, was responsible for his death."

It did seem likely. I doubted that the bag contained a half-eaten sandwich instead of a gun. And the old man had, after all, written out some sort of confession. And yet... there were these nagging doubts. Was this old, frail man really a murderer? That was the million-dollar question.

12

I would have said that nothing about the Mobius case could surprise me anymore. But that turned out to be wrong. The most fantastic twist was yet to come.

It came in shape of a visitor to my office. It was a foggy California morning. I drove through the mist to my office. The big green velvety hills, which form a kind of spine down the peninsula, were all shrouded in gray. Mornings of this kind are chilly and even a bit depressing. But by noon, the sun burns the fog off and life is bright and serene again. I was in a good mood by eleven, especially since the mail had brought in a couple of excellent checks from excellent clients.

The visitor—or rather visitors—were completely unexpected. There were two of them: a man and a woman. The woman was in her late 30's, I would say, or perhaps early 40's, with bleached blonde hair, rather stiff and piled on top of her head. She wore garish lipstick, and dark eye shadow. All this made her seem, dare I say it, harsh and common. The most salient thing about her physically was her belly: she was obviously pregnant. She sat down ponderously, as women do in the late stages of pregnancy. Throughout the conversation, she kept stroking her belly, as if she was trying somehow to calm down the raucous little imp inside of her.

The man seemed somewhat older. He was maybe 50, perhaps a bit more, of average height, average build, hair slightly gray. He had a somewhat shifty look. Or was I imagining this?

"Yes?" I said, to the two of them.

She said: "You're Frank May."

"Guilty as charged."

"My name is Wanda Skadden. I'm from Australia. And this is my partner, Dennis Little. He's also from Australia."

She had indeed a strong Australian accent. I think Dennis did too. But she did almost all of the talking, so I didn't have that much to go on, as far as Dennis was concerned.

"I understand you're handling the estate of Simon Mobius," she said.

"That's true."

"I also understand," she said, "that the estate is due to inherit a substantial sum of money from Rupert Mobius, the brother of Simon Mobius."

"Yes, that's correct," I said. "Rupert Mobius had a large estate. And his brother, Simon Mobius, was a substantial heir. As you said, I'm handling the estate. May I ask whether you have some business with the estate?"

She ignored my question, and asked one of her own. "So you've received a great deal of money, right?"

"Well, in fact," I said, "nothing has yet actually come in. The estate... well there are complications, which I prefer not to go into."

"I also understand that a large sum of money was left to Piers Mobius."

"Well, that's also correct. But, as I believe you know, Piers Mobius is dead. He died in a boating accident. Off the coast of Australia. I don't know the exact date, but it was before either his uncle or his father had died."

"His money goes to his children, am I right about that?"

"Well, yes. Piers Mobius had a son and a daughter, yes. They're my clients. They'll inherit whatever would have gone to their father... or their grandfather, for that matter."

"A son and a daughter," she said. "But you're not quite accurate there. There are or will be two sons. Two sons of Piers Mobius."

I said: "As far as I know, there's only one son. My client, Derek Mobius."

"And what about Piers Mobius, Jr.?" she said, with a smirk; and she exchanged a look with Dennis that I could only describe as gleeful and somehow malicious.

"Excuse me," I said, "who is Piers Mobius, Jr.? Where does he live? And why has nobody ever heard of him, including me."

"Oh, he lives right here," she said, rubbing her belly, and smirking again.

"Excuse me?"

"What I'm saying is, he hasn't been born yet."

"Not born yet?"

"You can see, I'm pregnant, can't you? Well, that's Piers Mobius' baby. I was very close to Piers Mobius. Piers and I, we had great times, if you know what I mean. I don't have to draw you a picture. Oh, that was before I met Dennis," she said, grinning, squeezing Dennis' knee, and winking at him. "Piers and I were an item, as they say. And this is his baby," she said, stroking her belly again. "It's a boy, by the way. I had an ultrasound. I'm going to name him Piers Mobius, Jr."

"But, excuse me, Ms. Skadden," I said. "I don't have to remind you, but Piers Mobius... he's been dead for over a year...."

"You think I don't know that? I've been around the block a few times. I know the facts of life. But Frank, you know, this is the modern world. I'm going to call you Frank. You can call me Wanda. A man doesn't have to be alive to become a father. He can be as dead as a doornail, but his sperm lives on. I suppose you know this. It's not just the birds and the bees any more. I'm carrying the baby of Piers Mobius. And he's going to be a very rich little boy. Am I right? He's going to come in for a big fat share of his father's estate and his grandfather's."

I was flabbergasted. "You say.... You're pregnant, well, obviously you are; but you're claiming that the father... is somebody who's dead?"

"I'm not 'claiming,' I'm telling you. Piers Mobius is the father of this child."

"And... you used, uh, artificial insemination...?"

"I did."

"I mean," I said, fumbling for words, "it wasn't, uh, sex, but...."

"Don't you get what I'm saying? I know it's not on the bar exam, but still, you don't have to be a rocket scientist to understand. Of course the man is dead. I wasn't making love to a corpse. Not that there's a corpse around. Piers Mobius is fish food, as you know. And, believe me, it's a lot more fun making love with live people, isn't it Dennis?"

"Wanda...," he said, embarrassed. Can't say I blamed him.

She ignored him. "Oh, yes, dead people aren't the least bit sexy, I mean, unless you have some kind of kinky thing, which is certainly not me, not this girl, oh no. Live ones are better, a lot better than a turkey-baster or whatever. I have to say, though, that in this case, I almost had an orgasm, I was so excited. I mean, I said to myself, Wanda, you're not just injecting a bunch of little sperm cells, you're injecting millions and millions of dollars. Ooh, I tell you, that was *so* erotic. So, yes, this is the child of Piers Mobius, and my little honey is going to be worth a lot of money when he's born."

I hardly need to tell you how much I was surprised— taken aback—by all this; and for a while I felt mentally paralyzed. Could this possibly be true? Was this woman really carrying the baby of Piers Mobius? And if she was, *would* that baby inherit, along with Derek and his sister? I mumbled something at least to indicate that, assuming her story was correct, I was not at all sure about these, uh, latter day babies, whether they inherited or not, and I would have to look into it very carefully, and so on.

"Oh, don't bother," she said, patting her belly once more. "We checked it out with the lawyers, didn't we, Dennis?" I looked at him. He said nothing. He had a wan smile on his face. I wondered what he was thinking.

I kept on muttering something about the law being unsettled. I vaguely remember reading a column on the web or in some lawyer magazine about this issue. I paid very little attention at the time. I had not yet encountered the sex life of the dead.

The discussion, in any event, was basically at an end. She had come to my office, she said, simply to inform me as lawyer for the estate that there was another heir just over the horizon. "Come, Dennis," she said, triumphantly; and the two of them swept out, leaving me sitting and staring out the window. I rued the day I ever got mixed up with the Mobius clan. But it was too late now for regrets.

13

Of course, I had to pass on this news to my clients, Derek and Doris. I thought about how to communicate these remarkable developments. I could say: there's good news and bad news. The good news is this: you're going to have an addition to your family circle. Or at least this is a possibility. The bad news is, it promises to be expensive and disruptive. But I was sure Derek and Doris would not be amused. I decided I had to give it to them straight.

The two of them were sitting in my office, and they sat stock still and wide-eyed, as I told them everything about Wanda Skadden's visit. First came shock and then anger. Well, anger on the part of Doris: she was furious. Derek, once the news began to register, seemed to find the idea intriguing.

"A new brother? Hey, Dodo, now that I think about it, it's kind of exciting. Who would have thought?"

But she shut him up quickly. "Derek, how could you? It's a pack of lies. This woman is just after our money."

"Well, some of it," he said. "A third of it. We'll still be rich, if this miserable estate ever gets disentangled."

"Derek," she said. "Sometimes I wonder about you. You forget I *know* something about this woman. She's a fraud, she's as crooked as a three-dollar bill! She's always been a fraud. This whole thing is an elaborate scam. She did have an affair with our father, I know that. But this ridiculous story about carrying his child—come on! She knows that our father is at the bottom of the Pacific

Ocean, and that there's no body, no DNA or anything like that, and she thinks she can get away with this. I don't think for one second that this unborn child belongs to our family. She's probably angling for some sort of cash payment, I mean it's blackmail. Frank, can't you do something about this?"

"Me? What can *I* do?"

"You can investigate this woman. Expose her. She's a complete fraud, believe me."

Of course I agreed to do nothing of the sort, though I was polite about it: after all, Doris was a client. I told her I never did investigations, which was basically true. I don't do investigations for a living: I'm not Sam Spade or any other private eye. But occasionally, when something tickles my fancy, I'm not beyond a little bit of cautious digging. Still, ferreting out the truth about Wanda Skadden was definitely not something I could do, or was willing to do. Doris left with a stern and determined look on her face. I was sure I had not heard the last of this issue.

14

When Doris and Derek left, I leaned back in my chair and began thinking. I realized that I was spending a lot of time on the Mobius estate, and it was not at all clear that anybody would ever pay me for my efforts... or pay me adequately. There are fee scales for estates set by law, but if there's something special about an estate, something not in the usual line, you can petition the Probate Court for "extraordinary fees." Probate lawyers do this all the time. Sometimes I think that they consider it extraordinary to do any work whatsoever. I'm more cautious myself. But in this case, I certainly would ask for more.

Assuming, that is, that the money materialized at all. Which was not at all sure.

I had nothing against Derek and Doris; they seemed like perfectly decent people on the whole. But I wish I had never had to deal with the whole Mobius clan, and I'm sure Gideon shared my views.

Ah, Gideon. As I was musing, the phone rang, and I heard Ms. Guthrie's voice: "Mr. Grambling would like to speak to you." I'm sure I lost caste—if I had any caste left to lose—by answering my own phone. Then the great man got on the phone and asked me to come see him at his office. He had a meeting scheduled with the infamous Fern Plotnick, and he wanted me to be there.

He told me that he was going to try to convince Fern Plotnick to step down as executor and trustee. She was clearly unsuited for these tasks. So are a lot of people, I said to myself, but most of them at least follow directions. But I could understand it if Gideon thought Fern Plotnick would simply be impossible. He wanted to replace her with himself or, if that didn't work, with Derek, who was after all a close relative and seemed reasonably sane. There were closer relatives, of course—Katerina and Cranshaw—but Gideon thought he could convince a judge that since they were suing the estate, it would be clearly wrong to put them in charge of it. If all else failed, he wanted to try to persuade Fern Plotnick to allow him to serve as co-trustee and co-executor. He was sure the court would go along.

He told me all this while we were waiting for Fern Plotnick, who ultimately came forty-five minutes late. This was extremely annoying. Obviously, Gideon pre-ferred to have people wait for him, and here the tables were turned. Fern, when she appeared, was dressed in high-class bag-lady style—a long flowered skirt, support hose, dirty sneakers. Gideon, after some small talk, which she totally ignored, went right to the point. He spoke to her in his most gentle and oily voice: He asked whether she really wanted to serve as executor and trustee. It was a great deal of work and extremely technical as well as time-consuming, and so on. He should have added that it came with a nice fee, but he left that part out. She had the right to resign, or rather not to accept the position in the first place, which was something that was done all the time (he said). The probate court would then appoint someone else, perhaps him, he said, who would take this crushing burden off her shoulders.

But Gideon got absolutely nowhere. Fern Plotnick was adamant. "It's my duty," she said. "Rupert wanted me to do this. He told me it was my duty."

I had said nothing at all up to that point. Gideon fi-nally gave up, in disgust, and retreated into his office. He barely managed to maintain his composure and avoid alienating Fern Plotnick. Anyway, I had the feeling that she was so self-absorbed she had no idea of how Gideon

Grambling felt.

When Gideon left, I left too, and Fern Plotnick followed me out the door. We got into the elevator together. I felt she was staring at me. It was a bit disconcerting. I gave her a sickly smile. We got out at the lobby, and she suddenly turned and said to me: "I don't trust that man. He's evil."

I said nothing.

She said: "His name is Gideon. He's a bad person. Gideon is a name bad people might have. You're a good person. Your name is Frank. I think names mean things. I think people become what their names tell them to be. I've become more and more like a fern. In tune with nature."

"Oh yes," I said.

It was one of those cold, sterile lobbies, all marble and modernist paintings, with two huge potted palms, and some starkly chrome and leather chairs. She sat down on one of the chairs, and motioned me to sit down on another one. "You, I can talk to," she said. "You have a nice face. I don't think you want to harm me. Or Rupert, poor soul. He made so many mistakes."

"Oh, we all do," I said, stumbling for some response. But I thought: if she trusts me, maybe I can get some information out of her. Information, I have to confess, that had little to do with running the estate; but about things that were on my mind.

"Ms. Plotnick, I'm so glad you trust me. I do appreciate that. My job is to help you. Help the estate. I want to help to, uh, carry out what Rupert wanted."

"If we only could," she said. "That man stands in the way, and those two awful children of his, I mean, Rupert's."

"Can I ask you," I said, summoning up my courage, "did you have a key to the apartment? To Mr. Mobius' apartment."

"Yes, I did. He gave it to me. He said, Fern, you need

a key to the apartment, I want you to be able to come and go. Come and go. That's what he said. Come and go."

"Well, did you come and go very often?"

"When I was needed."

"And... can I ask, did you go into the apartment at all, on the day he died?"

"Oh yes," she said. "I went. Because I knew something was wrong. I had a vision, a premonition.... The spirits were talking to me, and I knew that something terrible was going to happen. So I was worried. I took my key and I opened the door. The air was... thick with fearful things. There were two people there, with Rupert. An old man, and a younger man. They were sitting there, and I smelled danger. The old man was his brother. I don't know who the other man was. Rupert asked me to leave. I didn't want to, and I took him aside, and I said, these men are dangerous, but he told me he knew what they wanted and he could handle it."

"What time was that? Do you remember?"

"I never keep track of time. I don't like clocks. I feel that clocks are bad. Especially clocks that tick. I have no clocks in my house."

I nodded my head, as if I too was a member of the anti-clock cult. "Did you leave the apartment, Ms. Plotnick? When Rupert asked you to?"

"Yes. I had to. I stood outside in the hall and I heard shouting, anger, bad words. I knew this would end up the wrong way, but there was nothing I could do. I went back into my room. I live across the hall, right across from Rupert's place. I listened to the shouting, and I was afraid of what might happen."

"What were they saying?"

"I don't know. Talking about money, I think. Wills. Rupert's will.... I don't like those things either. They're messages from the living to the dead, and from the dead to the living."

"Can you be a bit more specific? What were they saying about wills?"

But she shook her head, no. Either she didn't know; or she didn't feel like telling me. I plunged boldly on:

"Somebody shot Mr. Mobius. Did you hear the shot?"

"Yes, I heard it."

"Was it before or after the two men left?"

"I don't know. I can't remember. I didn't see them leave. I heard the noise. I wasn't sure it was a gun. I don't really know what guns sound like. I hate guns. I waited a bit, I don't know how long. Then I went back into the room. There was nobody there, and he was lying on the floor. He was dead. And the phone rang. Something inside of me said, pick up the phone."

"And?"

"It was a woman calling him. I said hello and she hung up. I was frightened. Who was that woman? I had a feeling of dread. I was shaking like a leaf. I felt, I have to get out."

"Did you see a gun?"

"No. I saw nothing. But I heard voices."

"Voices?"

"The spirits were talking.... I could sense their presence in the room, but I couldn't see them. They told me to be quiet and not to touch anything.... Maybe one of the voices was Rupert's voice. He was a spirit by then. I think it was his voice. Anyway, the spirits told me not to call the police. They told me to go back to my place, and stay there until the spirits gave me further instructions. I sat there waiting and waiting. A long time went by. I didn't know what to do."

"And, you say, there was nobody in the apartment? When you went back in?"

"Rupert was there. Lying on the floor. I could see that he was dead. I saw nobody else. Maybe somebody was there, I didn't go into other rooms. I don't think anybody was there. But I don't know. I only heard those voices."

"Voices? More than one?

"I don't remember. Maybe." And then she looked at me, with a suspicious, crafty look on her face. "You don't believe a word I'm saying," she said. "Was I wrong about you? Are you like all those other people?"

"Oh no, Ms. Plotnick. I believe every word. Honor bright," I said.

This seemed to reassure her. She went on: "The next day, I went back into the apartment. There were noises and people all over. There were these policemen, and they asked me so many questions. I told them nothing. I didn't trust them. They were big, big men, with red faces. I didn't like them: they carried guns. I said I saw and heard nothing. I heard them talking about me, they said things like, crazy old woman. They asked me to look around, let them know if there was anything missing. I said, no, nothing, nothing is missing."

"I guess they thought it might be a burglar, I mean, the person who killed Mr. Mobius; that's why they were asking."

"Oh, no, there was something else on their mind," she said. "They couldn't fool me. That's why I lied to them."

"You lied?"

"Oh yes, something was missing."

"What was it?"

She leaned over, and spoke in a hoarse whisper, as if to prevent anybody from hearing what she was saying: "The photo album...."

"Photo album?"

"Oh, yes," she said. "He had a photo album. And last year, he bought another camera. Maybe he had a camera before. I don't know. But this was a special camera. A camera with special powers. I warned him about it, but he didn't listen to me."

"Special powers?"

"That's what I believe. I believe, and Rupert did too, that a good camera can see things the human eye can't see.... You know, dogs can hear noises people can't hear.

There are things animals can see that we can't see; but the camera can do this, it's like an animal, only it isn't. I believe you can see the soul when it leaves the body. I mean, you can't see it, but it's there, and animals can see it, dogs, that's why a dog barks when its master dies, and this camera, I truly believe, this was a camera that could do that."

"Is the camera gone?"

"I don't know. I didn't look for it. But the album, that was gone. I looked for it, and it was gone. I think the camera was gone, too."

"Why would somebody take a photo album?"

She looked me straight in the face. "I'll tell you why. The somebody who took it was not necessarily a human being, I mean, not an ordinary human being. There were spirits sometimes in Rupert's apartment. And I think whoever killed him took a picture of him, a picture of his spirit leaving his body.... Something we can't see, a kind of hazy cloud. And that's why they're both gone, the camera and the album. I firmly believe that. I think the album had... these pictures, these kinds of pictures...."

"Ms. Plotnick, did you, personally, ever *see* this album? Did you ever look inside of it, to see what kind of pictures, photos, were in there?"

"No. He didn't want me to see that album. He used to put it away in a drawer when I came in. I know that's what he wanted, and I respected that. But," she added, "I think that's why he had to die."

"Could you... I mean, could you explain that? He had to die because of the album?"

"Maybe it's dangerous to take pictures like that," she said. "Maybe one of the spirits, one of the souls, became angry."

The woman is totally insane, I thought to myself. Of course, Gideon is right: she absolutely cannot run the estate, manage the trust, or do any of these things. I sympathized with his desire to get her removed. But it wasn't going to be easy.

"Do you believe me, Mr. Frank?"

"Oh yes," I said, putting on my most sincere-looking face. If all this wasn't so absurd, it would be laughable. The notion of ghosts or spirits running around with re-volvers, shooting people, is ridiculous. It's not my image of a ghost anyway, not that I believe in ghosts. Or in photographs of the soul leaving the body.... But still, I had to wonder: was there *something* significant in her story? Should I dismiss the whole thing as garbage, or was that tiny, addled brain on to something? After all, she had been in the apartment; she had heard an argument; she heard a gunshot; and she saw two men talking to Rupert: Simon and somebody else.

I felt it was important to stay on the good side of Fern Plotnick. I kept smiling and nodding my head as she rattled on. Then she got up to go. "You don't have a car, do you?" I asked. She shook her head no. "I'll walk," she said. "I like to walk. I walked all the way here."

"But it's miles and miles," I said. "You're tired. Let me drive you."

She seemed reluctant; but she finally agreed. I tried to make conversation on the way, with little success. But when I deposited her at the entrance to her apartment building, I said, "It's been nice talking to you, Ms. Plotnick," and she smiled right back at me.

That evening was a particularly quiet night at home. After dinner, Celia did paperwork from the high school classes she was teaching. The girls were off at friends' houses. I had a chance to sit back in an easy chair and go over in my mind what Fern Plotnick had told me. When you subtracted the camera, the spirits, the hazy cloudlike souls, there was something quite definite left behind, something that couldn't just be the product of her fevered imagination. She said there were two men in the apartment talking to Rupert Mobius—and arguing with him, perhaps. An old man, and a younger man. She identified the old man: Simon Mobius. But the younger man? Who could that be?

And what did she mean by "younger"? Did she mean actually young, or what? Fern Plotnick herself was not exactly young. Old people, I've noticed, people past 65 or so, have trouble distinguishing between people who are 50 and people who are 40 or even 35. Fifty is young to them.

It works the other way around, too. My friend Harold Inselbaum, a periodontist who lives down the block, is about 50, and turning a bit gray. He loves movies, and ever since his second wife, Hetty, ran off with another dentist and filed for divorce, he goes to the movies at least twice a week. He steps up to the box office, and says "senior" in a loud voice. You are supposed to be 65 to get the senior discount. But the kids who sell the tickets are teenagers, and to them, anybody over 30 qualifies as a senior. They honestly can't tell the difference. Nobody has ever asked Harold to show his ID. So who could this "younger" person be? Two candidates immediately came to mind: Derek Mobius, who really was young, and Gideon Grambling, whom she had just met and perhaps did not recognize.

Both Derek and Gideon denied they actually went up to the apartment. But people have been known to lie. Indeed, they seem to lie to *me* with some frequency.

15

The Mobius home was a one-story ranch house, in south Palo Alto, on a leafy and quiet street lined with a whole cluster of one-story ranch houses very much like the Mobius house. The grounds looked neat, middle-class, and well-tended. I dropped in on the family in the late afternoon. I had never met Mrs. Mobius, the mother of Derek and Doris, a handsome woman in her late 50's; we exchanged a few words and then she excused herself.

Doris thanked me for coming, offered me coffee, which I refused, and then got right down to business. The business was Wanda Skadden, and her pregnancy. Doris was indignant; I had never seen her so enraged. "That woman! I know who she is. She thinks she can get away with this."

"You've met her?"

"No, never. But I've heard a lot about her, and believe me, she's a piece of work. It's true, she did have an affair with my father; I knew that, that part is true. But the rest of this cock and bull story. I mean, really Frank; this woman comes here, she's pregnant, fine and dandy, she's got her live-in lover with her, and she has the colossal gall to suggest that the child is... well, you heard her."

"Don't you think it's really our baby brother, Dodo?" Derek said, and laughed.

"It's not funny, Derek," she said. "She's no fool. She knows that there's no body, she knows that father is at the bottom of the ocean, she knows, or *thinks* she knows, that nobody can prove she's wrong. She'll swear on a stack of Bibles, she'll bring in documents, God knows what else. But I'm not going to take this lying down. I've already started investigating."

"Doris can be a ball of fire," Derek said to me. "This woman will be sorry she ever started in with us."

"I want you to help us, Frank," she said. "I've already made contacts in Australia: I'm looking into this pretty thoroughly. But I want you to talk to Wanda. You can do it. Make nice to her, if you know what I mean. Find out how come she has, or claims to have, sperm cells from our father. I mean, where did she get them, and why?"

"Why me?" I asked.

"She came to you," Doris said. "I think she maybe trusts you. You can tell her you represent the estate, which is true, and that we're your clients, which is also true. But that if this really is the child of Piers Mobius, it's an heir, and it'll be also your client, that is, it'll share in the estate, and so on. You'll know how to do this."

I found the idea a bit distasteful, but I had to agree on one point: if this was the child of Piers Mobius, then, yes, it would be an heir or a potential heir, and it would be my client. So I agreed to talk to Wanda Skadden again, and try to find out more details. Doris seemed pleased. "I'll take that coffee now," I said.

I did my duty. Wanda had left me a phone number and an address. I called Wanda, and made an appointment to see her the next morning at 9:30.

The address turned out to be a motel on El Camino Real, which runs down the spine of the peninsula. El Camino Real in Spanish means the royal road, but in our part of the state there's not much about it that seems royal. The street is lined with strip malls, branches of McDonald's and Burger King, tired little motels, and Chinese restaurants with names like Golden Dragon. El

Camino does have its gentrified moments when it passes through posh suburbs with their leafy streets from which all commerce has been banned, but for the most part it's a depressing wasteland of commerce.

Wanda's motel was in Mountain View, just to the south of Palo Alto. It was called the Royal Road Motel, in honor of the street I suppose. It was clearly *not* a destination of choice for venture capitalists, businessmen from Singapore, Silicon Valley executives, or brain surgeons from Santa Monica visiting their children at the Stanford Business School. It had a sad little swimming pool on one side, big enough (it seemed to me) only for children under five. The motel was a two-story affair. Business seemed only so-so, judging from the small number of cars parked in front. None of them was a Mercedes. In front of the motel was a small office and a sign that announced that there were, in fact, vacancies.

I parked and went into the office. Inside was a desk, a chair or two, and three potted plants with unhappy, drooping leaves. A young Asian woman sat inside behind the counter, reading *People* magazine. I mentioned Wanda Skadden's name, and asked her to call. She yawned, put down the magazine, and made the call.

Wanda appeared rather promptly, waddling awkwardly and stroking her belly somewhat obsessively. She was alone. "Dennis is still asleep," she explained. "He needs his sleep." She failed to specify exactly *why* he needed his sleep. We all do need sleep, I suppose, including Dennis.

We were obviously not going to talk in the office of the Royal Road Motel. Wanda suggested Starbucks, which was less than a block away. Starbucks is always less than a block away. She ordered a skimmed-milk latte. I had a cup of coffee and—giving way to weakness—a blueberry scone. We found a place in the corner which was reasonably private. It was early in the day: most of the engineering students with laptops had not yet arrived.

"Wanda, we need to talk," I began.

"I have things to talk to *you* about," she said.

"As you know," I said, "I represent the estate...."

"Yes, yes," she said, with a certain amount of impatience. "We've been through all that. Really, I'm not an idiot, you don't need to repeat yourself. I know who your clients are."

"I've been speaking to, uh, my clients. I mean Derek and Doris Mobius...."

"Your clients. Yes. But don't forget Piers Mobius, Jr.!" she said, with a triumphant smirk on her face.

"Hold on," I said. "Maybe you're right. Maybe. If this is actually a child of the deceased...."

"Which it is."

"Then it *may* have a right to share in the inheritance. I said 'may,' because the legal rules are obscure. This isn't a usual situation: I hope you understand that."

"My little boy is going to get his money," she said. "I'll fight like a tiger for him. I'm a real tiger mom, believe me."

I believed her. But I stumbled on about how the law wasn't entirely settled, there aren't many cases, and they don't all agree, and it depends on which state you're in, and so on.

She waved her hands in the air, to indicate her disdain. "Cases, cases! Well, they'll see what they're up against, when it's me that's involved. And my little darling baby!"

I shuddered to think of what might happen to someone who got in her way, including me. But I went on anyway: I had to. "You won't be surprised to hear that, uh, the other children are a bit dubious and suspicious...."

"Naturally," she said, "Did I expect them to throw their arms around me and hug me? No, indeedy. Not if I was going to cost them millions of dollars, oh no, there'll be no love lost. I'm the wicked stepmother. But I don't care: I can take it, I'm tough as nails." She bent her head and whispered, more or less in the direction of her navel,

"I'll see to it that you're rich, my little boy."

"And here's the thing," I said. "You say this is the child of Piers Mobius. But can you prove it? He's not around to help us out, and there's no body, no DNA. I mean, it's just your word that the, uh, sperm belonged to Mr. Mobius. People don't go around collecting that sort of thing, I mean, even from intimate friends."

"We were lovers," she said. "Everybody in Australia knew that."

"Well, I suppose that's true," I said. "But... you're not lovers now, I mean, since he's dead. And yet you claim.... I mean, how is it you had his, uh, genetic material? That isn't the usual thing to do, is it?"

I felt at sea here in my bland little suburban world. Maybe collecting sperm was all the rage these days. Who knows what this generation is up to? Kids, I understand, send nude pictures of themselves on their little smartphones; maybe exchanging sperm samples was the custom in certain sets.

"I guess you don't know about my business back-ground. I was in the sperm business," she said.

"Excuse me? The sperm business?"

"Yes, the business of collecting sperm. I had this plan, it was a wonderful business model. Wonderful. I was going to collect sperm from famous men: Nobel prize winners, scientists, movie stars, big athletes, you know, basketball players or swimmers or whatever, and then I would sell this stuff to women who wanted great babies."

"And... did this work?"

"Not really. I'll be honest with you: I didn't make any money, and I had to give it up in the end. I guess my business model wasn't as great as I thought. The Nobel prize winners, they wouldn't cooperate; and it turned out they were all 90 years old and the worst sort of geeks, anyway. And the movie stars, they were hopeless; I made a real effort, but I suppose they were too high and mighty to be bothered. I did get some response from athletes, at least some of them; I mean, not the top-drawer athletes, the ones who make millions of dollars, they don't give away their sperm, they do it the natural way, if you know what I mean—but I got some footballers to cooperate, some college jocks, some basketball players, and one absolutely gorgeous rugby player. But it wasn't enough for the business to get going. And, to tell you the truth, a lot of those jocks said, sure, you can have my sperm, but not in a cup, how about it, honey, that sort of thing."

"But Piers Mobius," I said, "he wasn't exactly a star athlete now, was he?"

"Oh no," she said. "As far as *his* sperm is concerned, well, I don't have to draw you a picture, do I? You're over 21, so you know what we were up to. Over 21—that's a laugh," she said. "That's from the Dark Ages, when kids hardly knew about the birds and the bees. Nowadays, you could say, over 14! I could tell you stories about high school boys! Anyway, you're right. He was no star. But Piers, anyway, he did want me to add him to my collection. He had his reasons. Piers had premonitions.... He had all sorts of enemies, he said, people who had it in for him. He was terribly afraid of dying. We didn't want children, but he said eventually he thought, maybe he would want a child. After all, he said, he wanted to carry on the line."

I thought that was odd. The line was already carried on in the form of Derek and Doris, and Piers Mobius never showed the slightest interest in them. I pointed this out to her.

"You're right," she said, after a short pause. "I was telling you a little bit of a fib. It wasn't about children at all. He wanted life after death."

"Life after death?"

"Well, more or less. He thought science would work out a way to bring people back, with the DNA, you know; and he thought, well, sperm would be the best thing for that. He wanted to have his body frozen too, put in some kind of deep freeze, you know, so that he could be revived when science made it possible. Poor man, that didn't happen because of the way he died."

"Does sperm have your DNA? Could you make some sort of a clone with it? I mean, is that even theoretically possible?" I had no clue about any of this. It was 25 years or more since I took a biology course in college. I had no aptitude for it, then or now, and, anyway, I'm not sure they even knew what DNA was when I took the course. I hated the teacher, by the way.

Wanda shrugged her shoulders and patted her stomach again. She said: "Well, it didn't matter, did it? I'm not cloning the man, I'm just giving him a baby. He was part of my sperm collection, that's all. And then later on I met Dennis, and that was the end of Piers Mobius. I mean, Dennis wowed me. He swept me off my feet. The minute I met him, Piers Mobius didn't *exist* for me.... I found him so... inadequate. Dennis was the real McCoy. What a lover! He made Mobius look sick. So I told him: Piers, you're history. I think it was a real shock to him, big ego that he was. And maybe he really loved me. But I didn't care. There was nothing he could do. I was ready to move on, and that was that."

I almost felt some sympathy for the late Piers Mobius, even though from all accounts he was a first-class worm. The irony: First she dumped the man and now she's having his child out of sheer greed. "And when," I asked, "did you decide to, uh, have his baby?"

"It was Dennis' idea. Dennis is so full of good ideas! We were so madly in love, and I said to him, my darling Dennis, I want to have your baby. But Dennis said he couldn't have children, you know, a vasectomy. I said, oh, Dennis what a pity, you're an alpha male, you should have children, but he just laughed. But then he said, let's have a baby anyway; and that's where the idea came from."

There was, I thought to myself, something dramatically wrong with this story. If she had a collection of genetic material from athletes and who knows who else, why would they choose to reproduce Piers Mobius, her ex-boyfriend, whom she no doubt despised and who she had dumped unceremoniously? Yes, the baby was now a ticket to millions of dollars. But how could she have known that? She looked to me to be late along in her pregnancy—maybe her eighth or ninth month. When she became pregnant, was Rupert Mobius already dead?

I felt I needed to check the chronology. Later I did this as carefully as I could. Rupert Mobius had died in January. Derek came to see me in October, and it was now December with the baby not yet born.

So... she probably became pregnant *after* Rupert died—fairly soon after, as a matter of fact. I didn't dare ask her the date she used the turkey-baster. This was only one of many questions I couldn't ask. Did she know that Rupert Mobius had left a fortune to Piers Mobius and his descendants? Was she in this country or in Australia at the time?

Doris had hired a private investigator to look into the affairs of Wanda Skadden. I was dying to know what this person would turn up. I soon found out.

16

Curiosity is one of my worst traits. Or one of the most endearing: take your pick. I called Doris as soon as Wanda left my office. She was out, so I left a message on her answering machine.

Days went by. Doris, it seems, was waiting for a report. When she got it, she called me and we arranged to meet in my office.

"Well," I said. "Did your guy find anything?"

"Oh, quite a bit," Doris said. She was smiling broadly. "We really got results. Some of it was quite a surprise."

"Tell me, Doris. I love surprises. Well good ones anyway."

"This is such a weird story," she said. "I'll tell you the truth, if it wasn't for the money, or should I say, the chance of losing the money, which makes it a bit tense, I think I'd positively enjoy all of this. Did you know, for instance, that Rupert Mobius had been drawing lots of money from his bank accounts? Something on the order of $40,000. Over a period of some weeks. And only a few days before he died, he drew out another $10,000."

"Do you know why?"

"Not a clue. So where did the money go? He certainly didn't spend it on himself, the old goat. He didn't invest it...."

"How do you know that?" I asked. "Couldn't he have decided to buy stocks and bonds or whatever? Money in the bank these days pays almost nothing: a man like

111

Rupert would be looking for a better investment."

"I checked with Gideon. By the way, getting information out of *him* is like pulling teeth. But whatever. He's been compiling the estate's inventory, so I spoke to him and also to the broker Rupert used. He hadn't made any new investments, oh, for months. Nothing at all."

"So what's your theory, Doris? What's this all about?"

"The money certainly wasn't in the apartment, at least not when people looked at every inch of the place," she said. "So where was it? Was it stolen?"

"Stolen? By whom?"

"Well, there are a number of possibilities," she said. "The first is a burglar. Now I know the police, and everybody else, don't think somebody broke into the apartment and stole stuff. But that's because we thought nothing was missing. Maybe he had a lot of cash in the apartment, and that's what the guy took. So maybe it's time to bring back the burglar idea."

"But remember," I said, "there were no signs of burglary at all, no signs of a break-in. And why would a burglar decide on this particular apartment, in a run-down building in a crummy neighborhood? He'd have to know about the cash. And then, think of Rupert's psychology. Would a man like that really keep wads of cash in his house instead of in the bank? Doesn't make sense. So what's the next possibility, Doris?"

"Theory B is Fern Plotnick."

"Fern Plotnick? You can't be serious."

"Why not? Because she seems like a harmless crazy old lady? So what? How much does it take to lift a wad of bills out of a drawer? You don't think she's up to it? She's poor as a church mouse, isn't she?"

"I suppose. It just doesn't seem in character," I said.

"Well, nothing about Rupert, life or death, makes any sense, isn't that true? So that means anything is possible."

I had to agree.

"To be honest," Doris said, "I don't really think Fern

Plotnick stole the money. But I can't rule it out. Anyway, that's not the biggest news, the money thing. It's the report from the private investigators, the ones that were looking into Wanda Skadden."

"Right."

Doris told me that her investigators ("they're costing me a ton of money, but it's worth it—I hope") were still working—both in California and in Australia—to find out more about "that woman." But they already had quite a lot, especially the trail of Wanda Skadden in Australia. And it was a substantial trail.

Wanda, it seems, had a long history of crooked dealing. The sperm business was only the latest in a long line of schemes. Yes, she did claim to have a sperm collection, she advertised that she could produce sperm from Nobel Prize winners and from great athletes, and the like: "Give your baby the best! The best brains, the best body—the best chance in life." None of this was even remotely true. Whatever material she had was gathered from medical students for the most part, for small sums of cash—and even they were misled into thinking they were donating to a charitable organization "for the relief of childless married women." What was most scandalous, however, was that Wanda also cultivated high school seniors. The details were murky but disreputable. She was gathering sperm from high school jocks, and there were rumors that she was also gathering sperm in more "conventional ways" from boys who were definitely underage. Threat of criminal prosecution was what made her decide, apparently, to leave Australia for the United States. With a new boyfriend in tow, Dennis Little.

"Wow, Doris," I said. "You almost have to admire her gall."

"I wanted to ask you a legal question," Doris said. "About extradition. Do you know anything about it? If she's wanted by the police, could we get her sent back to Australia? I'd dearly love that."

"What good would that do? She'd still give birth, and

she'd still make a claim on the estate."

"Maybe if we threatened her... frankly, we don't care about her rackets, the athletes, the medical students, or the high school kids. We only care about one possible donor: my father. Did she really have his sperm? Oh God," she added, "I can't believe I'm talking about this. His sperm. He was my father, after all! You know how people are, thinking about parents and sex. And here I am, talking about my father's sperm. It gives me the creeps, to be honest."

I nodded. Of course I understood. We all think we're the product of some kind of virgin birth. Anything else is too painful to contemplate.

"Anyway, the story gets complicated," she said, "as far as my father was concerned. Wanda was apparently quite something in her day, lots of men; but then she did seem to settle down with one guy. This was in Brisbane, and this is when Piers Mobius was living there. Anyway, this man she was with didn't call himself Piers Mobius, and he was a somewhat shadowy figure, but according to my sources, it was in fact my father. And he was in deep trouble. He had gotten a young girl pregnant, whose father was a rich businessman in Melbourne. The girl got an abortion, but Piers Mobius left town suddenly for Brisbane. That's where he connected with Wanda. God, to think that man is my father. *Was* my father, I should say."

"So...."

"So you see, Frank, it is in fact quite possible that she had a sperm sample from him. Why, I don't know. Maybe she was going to pass the stuff off as the product of a Nobel Prize winner. She was capable of anything."

I nodded in agreement again.

"On the other hand, she would have to preserve it, and I don't how they do that, what kind of facilities you have to use. I'm sure she didn't have anything more high-tech than her refrigerator. The whole thing was so crook-ed."

"So you don't believe her story?"

"I do not," Doris said. "The woman is a pathological liar and we'll prove it. She tells you this ridiculous story that Piers Mobius wanted the sperm saved so he could be resurrected, or whatever, and she expects us to believe it? Well, she probably doesn't; but she doesn't care, so long as she feels she can get away with it. When the baby is born, we'll do DNA testing. She's counting on the fact that Piers Mobius died in the middle of the Pacific and that we don't have a body. She'll swear by her mother's honor or something that she collected his sperm, that they were lovers; she'll bring in the evidence about his crazy ideas, about freezing himself and so on. She thinks we can't prove otherwise, and so we'll have to accept the baby as my father's or at least give her some gigantic settlement."

"But you can prove she's lying?"

"Yes! That's the beauty part! She was counting on fooling us. No body, no DNA. But I think we can show that she's a crook.""

"That's great. But how?"

"Maybe if Derek and I get tested—or maybe Derek is enough, I think that might show something. At least it could show that this baby couldn't be a relative of ours. But we've got something even better. I think. I'll know more about this later."

She added: "The woman is a fraud through and through. I think she just made up this sperm story. After she broke up with my father, she bounced around from town to town, took up with this Dennis person, and ultimately came to the States. Meanwhile, her scam, selling sperm from famous people, had just fallen apart. I can't believe that she was traveling from here to there, and all the time she had a jar or a plastic container or something. No, it doesn't make any sense. I think she knew that my father had a thing about death, and wanted to be frozen and so on, and when somehow she got wind of the money angle, she dreamed up this story. But we're going to prove she's a liar."

"Can you do that?"

"Absolutely."

Doris was clearly upbeat. She left my office in a very good mood. I wonder whether it was justified. Something about the whole story simply didn't compute. Could Wanda possibly be so brazen? I was beginning to develop a vague sort of hunch. It hung in my brain like a small cloud. But I couldn't quite put my finger on what it was.

17

I had to go to San Francisco on business a few days later, and I stopped off for lunch near Montgomery Street not far from the building where Gideon had his office. The restaurant was crowded, and I sat at the counter and ordered a bacon, lettuce, and tomato sandwich. A woman was sitting next to me. I was deeply engrossed in a book I was reading, a legal thriller, with a killer courtroom scene and I had hardly noticed her until she turned to me and said, "Mr. May?"

It was Ms. Guthrie, from Gideon's office. Her usual aplomb seemed to have vanished. I thought I saw streak marks on her cheeks, as if she had been crying. I said, "oh yes, Ms. Guthrie, how are you?"

"Terrible," she said. Of course I had to ask her why.

"I'm throwing my life away," she said. "People... think he's wonderful. A great lawyer. That's what you think, isn't it? Beautiful office in San Francisco. He makes money, oh, yes. Do you know how much that rug cost, the one in the conference room? It came from Armenia or someplace like that, hand-made. A whole village worked on it, women and children, it took them years. And he drives a Mercedes, a new one every year. His wife, she gets everything she wants. Goes to the beauty parlor twice a week. Sits at home and eats chocolates, I suppose. Plays bridge. And I... what's in it for me?"

I could smell what was coming.

"He promised me, he'd get a divorce. I said, Gideon,

I've heard that story before. He swore up and down. And now.... Now he says it's not possible, because of his daughter, the one who goes to Amherst. I said, Gideon, what has that got to do with anything? I don't care about Amherst, she's over 18, isn't she? He said he can't break up the family, not now. I said, no, just break me up, throw me away, like a used Kleenex, is that the idea?" Now the tears were flowing. I was deeply embarrassed. Why was she telling me this?

"But I have my pride," she said. "Maybe nothing else, but I have some pride. I won't lie for him: that's where I'm drawing the line. If he had been decent to me, but no...."

I nodded and tried to smile sympathetically.

"I was going to call you," she said. "It's my tiny little bit of revenge: telling you about his lies. It's not a nice thing to do, but I'm going to do it; I feel I have a right to do it, a right to get back at him. He lied to me, and he lied to you."

"He lied to me?"

"Oh yes. I tell you, he's scared to death. He doesn't want the police to know. He told you a story about Rupert Mobius. That he drove to the apartment building, but never went upstairs? That is nothing but a lie. I know, because I was driving the car."

"He said somebody drove him," I said. "He told me that. He had been to the optometrist, and his eyes were dilated."

She gave a hoarse, sad laugh. "The optometrist! Oh my God. *I'm* the optometrist. He had been to my condo. It was one of our little get-togethers. Our little love nest. Oh God, the stories he tells. And he tells you it was the op-tometrist. Oh Lord. What a fool I am."

I had no idea what to say. Tears began to flow again The waiter deposited my sandwich in front of me, and it sat there, saying "eat me." But somehow I felt it would be crude to bite into a sandwich, much as I wanted to, while this woman was pouring out her soul to me. I said "you mustn't blame yourself." This seemed like the right thing to say, for want of anything better. I was fidgeting in my seat. "It's not your fault," I said, which seemed bland enough for this situation.

The waiter brought her a salad. She stared at it, poked at it with a fork, took a mouthful, and then put the fork down. She seemed to be calmer than before. "I'm sorry I unloaded all this on you," she said. "I shouldn't have."

"Oh, no. Don't give it a moment's thought." She dabbed at her face with a tissue, took a few more bites, then left some money on the counter. "Please don't mention this to anybody," she said. "I'm really embarrassed. I lost my head."

"Not to worry," I said, giving her my most beatific smile. "But... he did go upstairs, then? He went to see Rupert Mobius?"

"Yes... but I shouldn't have told you. I just needed to tell somebody. Oh, not about that stupid Mobius person. About me and Gideon. What a fool I've been. But promise you won't say a word about this."

I promised.

"I still love him," she said. "He doesn't deserve it. I know he's taking advantage of me. But what can I do? I'm helpless. That's what love is like."

"Oh yes," I said.

She seemed calmer. "I have to get back to work," she said. Then she left, rather abruptly. I devoured my sandwich, and a dish of ice cream to boot.

I would never have dreamt in a million years that she and Gideon were having an affair. I suppose that shows how naïve I am. I had obviously caught her in a bad moment, some sort of crisis in that wretched relationship. But, as I drove back to my office, I thought about a kind of paradox: on the one hand, people seemed to confide in me, sometimes total strangers, or someone like Ms. Guthrie, who was almost a stranger; I didn't even know her first name. On the other hand, just as many people—and maybe more—seemed to lie to me all the time. Derek had definitely lied. And Gideon, I now realize, had also told me a whopping lie.

18

I tackled Gideon first. I had to indulge in a bit of lying myself, because I obviously wasn't about to reveal the source of my information. I arranged to have lunch with Gideon in San Francisco. I preferred not to go to his office and confront Ms. Guthrie at the front desk. Not now, anyway.

Everybody loves San Francisco. Tourists, that is. And people who live there. These two groups probably can avoid the problem of parking in the downtown area. When I have lunch in San Francisco, I often pay more for parking than for the lunch itself. I suppose it's the law of supply and demand. At any rate, we met in a dim, quiet fish restaurant not far from Gideon's office. We discussed some technical estate matters. I could tell that Gideon was suspicious: none of what we discussed obviously merited a trip to San Francisco. But I wanted to wait until the fish arrived on our plates before bringing up what was really on my mind.

"Gideon," I said, "I hate to have to say this. I really do. But you told me a story that, well, just wasn't exactly true."

"What are you referring to?" he said, with a note of indignation in his voice.

"You said you went to Rupert's apartment but that you stayed in your car the whole time."

"Yes, and?"

"Gideon, you went up the apartment: why didn't you

tell me that?"

"Frank, I have to ask you again: why is this any of your business? I don't notice a badge, are you a member of the police department suddenly?"

I had no real answer. "No, I am not a member of the police department. I just don't like... well, I just don't like it when somebody pulls the wool over my eyes."

"I see," he said, in an icy tone. "But even if it was your concern, which it most certainly is not, I don't see how you could possibly know what I did or did not do on that particular day. So, let's end this line of inquiry. Do I make myself clear?"

"Suppose I told you somebody saw you get out of the car and enter the building...."

"Indeed. And who could that be?"

"I'm not at liberty to say."

"And I'm not at liberty to comment. I don't believe you, anyway."

I felt it was time for a lie of my own. "All right: it was one of the neighbors, somebody who lives in the building. A married couple, in fact. They don't know you from Adam, but they said they saw a man get out of a black Mercedes and go in the front door...."

This seemed to produce an effect. He seemed genuinely taken aback. "And how is it that *you* are in possession of this information, if I might ask?"

"That is something I really can't tell you."

But Gideon clearly felt he was trapped. "Your source.... It isn't from the police? Are the authorities aware of this, uh, allegation?"

"No Gideon, they're not. Not yet."

"Not yet? But they will know eventually?"

"I don't think so. All this is quite confidential."

He seemed genuinely relieved. He paused, as if to think things over, and then he said: "Well, all right. Yes, Frank, I did go into the building. And I've lied about it. I told the police the same story I told you. I didn't want to be involved. I wasn't aware that there were, shall I say, witnesses. It could be quite embarrassing for me. I took a chance. I don't like to take chances, but I did in this case. But, Frank, I still feel aggrieved that you are, well, meddling in this whole affair. It is absolutely none of your business. How often do I have to tell you that?"

"Gideon," I said, "I'm sorry. But in a way it is my business. It's important to know what happened that day. Somebody killed the old man. I'm hoping it wasn't one of my clients. Or one of yours."

"Oh, that's preposterous," he said. "Ridiculous." But he knew it was far from ridiculous. We were both thinking the same thing: *somebody* killed Rupert Mobius. It wasn't a lightning bolt from heaven. It wasn't the spirits Fern Plotnick was always talking about. And that somebody might well be a client—his or mine.

Or Gideon himself?

We were quiet for a while. He tried to pretend he was concentrating on the grilled sole that sat on a plate in front of him. Was he reading my mind? He suddenly put down his knife and fork, looked at me and said: "All right. I've admitted I did get out of the car, and I did enter the building, yes. But do you seriously think I marched upstairs, killed my client, and marched right down again? Is that what you're hinting? If you are, that is truly, truly preposterous."

"I'm not hinting anything, Gideon. It's not good for business to kill clients. But by your own account, Rupert Mobius was the client from hell."

He relaxed a little. "Oh, too true, too true. If somebody held a gun to my head and said, you have to kill one client, or I'll kill you and your whole family, yes, my choice would definitely be Rupert Mobius. Nobody else would come close."

"And you did see him that day."

"No, I did not. I drove there because he had asked me to. I was extremely reluctant, as you know. And then, when I got there and went up to his apartment, the man seemed to have changed his mind. He wouldn't even let me in."

"You never went into the apartment?"

"No, never. I rang the doorbell, and he opened it up, after a couple of minutes, but only a crack; I couldn't even see into the room. I had the feeling there was somebody there, somebody else; for whatever reason, Rupert wanted to get rid of me. At the time I thought, maybe it's that lunatic, Fern Plotnick. I don't know why I thought so. I thought I heard voices. I can't really remember. I was just annoyed at the time, aggravated. Here I had swallowed my pride, driven to see him at home against my usual policies, and he's almost literally slamming the door in my face. I went back downstairs, fuming with rage. But now.... I do think this was important. Somebody was in there, maybe that Plotnick creature, but maybe somebody else too. Maybe it was the somebody who killed him."

"Did you see Simon, his brother? He was there that day."

"No. I saw nobody else."

"Did you notice a car parked right behind yours, in front of the apartment building?"

"Why would I? There were cars all over. It's a busy street. I suppose there was a car there. I just got in my car and drove away."

I guided the conversation back to estate matters. I noticed he had said nothing about Ms. Guthrie, the other person in his car. I felt this was best left alone.

Was Gideon telling the truth now, or was this just another lie? I had another wild idea: Ms. Guthrie zipped upstairs, murdered Rupert, and raced back down. I know, this makes no sense, but wouldn't that be a hoot? Her motive: revenge on Gideon, by robbing him of a lucrative client. Of course this was nonsense, but I played the scene in my mind with a certain amount of relish.

19

I tackled Derek next. He was sitting in my office, and here too I began by covering some details about the estate, what to do about overdue bills, how to manage the tax returns. Then I said to him, "Derek, I'm your lawyer. I'm on your side. You have to level with me. Don't you trust me?"

"Of course I do."

"Then why did you tell me something that isn't true?"

"Like what?"

"You told me that you just sat in the car the day your uncle died. Drove your grandfather, parked the car, and never went into the building. But in fact you did."

"How do you know that?" he said.

"Never mind."

"Doris told you," he said. "Must have been Doris. I wish she wouldn't do things like that. But all right, yes, I did go up."

"And?"

"I didn't actually go in. I rang the bell, I knocked on the door. At first nobody answered. Then my grandfather opened the door, just a crack. He said, Derek, go away. Don't come in. I said, why not. He said, just do as I say."

"Your grandfather? Simon Mobius? Not Rupert?"

"No. I never saw Rupert at all. You know, I had a feeling that something was very wrong, something was going on, why wouldn't he let me in? So I said, Grampa, is there a problem, can I help you? But he said no, nothing, just go away. Go back down and wait for me in the car. He wouldn't open the door, and he wouldn't let me in. I had the feeling there was somebody else there with him in the room, but it was just a feeling. I mean, somebody besides Uncle Rupert. I felt that this was not quite kosher, and I argued a little, but Grampa insisted: go away, go down, wait for me. So I did. I went down and sat in the car...."

"And then what happened?"

"Nothing. I mean, I already told you. Grampa came down, and he had this paper bag, and we dumped it in the ocean. That's all. And I wasn't lying; I never looked inside the bag. I swear it."

"And you think there was a gun in the bag."

"I guess. Look: Grampa wrote out this confession. Isn't that good enough for you? He was there, in the apartment, and he came down with this bag, and maybe there was a gun inside of it. End of story, no?"

But it wasn't.

20

Sometime in November, Wanda Skadden went into labor and produced a little boy. She gave me the news a day after she gave birth. "We're taking the little rascal home," she said. "I'm going to show him off. He's big and healthy. Wait till you see him."

And indeed, about a week later, she appeared at my office, together with her boyfriend Dennis.

She looked plumper than the last time I saw her. The baby was wrapped up in a blue and white cloth. It started to whimper, and she put it to her breast.

"Isn't it a little darling?" she said, and ceremoniously kissed the baby's head. "This is Piers Mobius, Jr. You're my little dumpling, aren't you?" she said, in a gushing voice addressed to the baby, which continued sucking, and otherwise ignored her. Dennis sat quietly at her side, occasionally stroking her shoulder.

I didn't quite know what to say. "Nice baby," I said, for what of anything better. To me, like many men, all babies seem the same.

"Seven pounds, ten ounces. And healthy as a horse," she said. "I knew it would be. You've got your mama's genes, too," she said to the baby. "Those are pretty strong genes, let me tell you. You'll be something in the world, I know you will."

"Have you, uh, been in touch with the family? I mean, the Mobius family?"

"I let them know the baby was born. Of course, they

were hoping it would die quietly or somehow just go away. But I fooled them," she said.

"As you know," I said, diffidently, "They don't really— how should I put it?—they don't really credit your story."

"You don't have to try to be diplomatic. I understand what they're thinking. They think I'm a fraud."

"Frankly, they do, Wanda. My clients say this is all a scam. This woman, she comes here, she has a boyfriend. How do we know it's not your boyfriend's baby?"

"Oh, what kind of a fool do you think I am? Of course I knew they would say that. Naturally they would. They'd try to say this is Dennis's baby—wouldn't they, dear?" she said, turning to Dennis, who seemed uncomfortable, but he nodded in agreement.

"Of course they're wrong," she said. "Dead wrong. When I decided to have Piers' baby, we didn't want anybody to even suggest such a thing, you know, that it was Dennis's, not Piers's. I was living with Dennis, yes. But we just stopped. No more sex. Even with the vasectomy. We had to be so careful! I said, Dennis, you're going to have to control yourself. We have to be like brother and sister. Separate beds, you know. That wasn't easy for me," she said, with a smirk. "I'm very passionate. I have deep feelings. Dennis is like that too," she added, squeezing his thigh. "Oh, I had to admire his patience, if you know what I mean."

He looked vaguely embarrassed: "Wanda...."

"Dennis said, can't we cheat, just a little? And I said: no way, Dennis. Too much at stake. You've just got to keep under control. Take a cold shower. Just be patient. Well, we managed. There was so much at stake! And as soon as it was confirmed, absolutely confirmed; as soon as I knew I was pregnant, and I got the news, we had a kind of second honeymoon."

"We never had a first one," Dennis said. "We're not married."

"Oh, Dennis, don't be so technical. You know what

I'm referring to," she said, as she pinched his thigh again. "You know, that weekend in Brisbane. If that wasn't a honeymoon, I don't know what was."

Dennis said nothing.

"And when I was sure I was pregnant," she said, "we had quite a time. We celebrated. We were in heaven. I mean, this was going to be a million-dollar baby."

"A lot more than a million," Dennis said.

"That was just a figure of speech," she said. The baby stopped sucking, whimpered a bit, and made gurgling noises. She put it on her shoulder, and patted the baby's back. "Oh, just like a honeymoon," she said. "We bought a bottle of champagne and we checked into a nice hotel, just like honeymooners. That lovely hotel in Brisbane. You remember, Dennis? Of course: how could you forget? We spent two whole days naked. I think I wore you out," she said.

He squirmed in his seat. "Wanda, please," he said.

"I don't care," she said. "Frank, look at him. Look at Dennis. You wouldn't think it, would you, but he's a powerhouse, he's a real tiger. I mean, he taught me things. I had Piers Mobius' baby inside me; but you know the truth? Piers Mobius, he was nothing. In bed, I mean. Big talk, no action, you know what I mean? Of course, he thought *he* was the tiger. Big macho blowhard. I tell you, it was more exciting getting pregnant with a turkey-baster, than having actual sex with that man. Now Dennis, here, he's quiet, but believe me, he's the real thing. Really endowed, if you know what I mean."

"Wanda, you talk too much," he said. He was scowling at her. "I have to warn you. Sometimes you go too far. People might get the wrong impression."

"Oh, Frank doesn't care, he's not shocked: he's heard it all," she said. "You lawyers, people tell you *everything*, I suppose. Family secrets, when it's a divorce or something like that. You get the real lowdown. Especially an attractive man like you, Frank. I'll bet your women clients can't keep their hands off of you! They're dying to tell you all about their sex lives, aren't they?"

"Not really...."

"Oh, never mind. Anyway, right after that weekend in Brisbane, we came to the United States. We flew first class. It cost a fortune, but it was worth it, wasn't it, Dennis? We had more champagne, they give it to you in first class, and we cuddled and toasted the future. I was feeling great, no morning sickness, nothing like that. And I felt I'm pregnant with *money*. I've got lots of money, right inside my belly. I thought, let the good times roll!"

He squirmed in his seat again. "Wanda, please," he said.

But there was no stopping her. "I always wanted money," she said. "Growing up, we didn't have any : not a pot to piss in, as the saying goes. There were five of us, and my dad was drunk all the time, I tell you, it was a struggle. I made a vow that someday I'll have money. And now, because of this sweet little baby, we'll have lots of money. Dennis and me, we'll get married. We'll go to Las Vegas and get married, Dennis and me and little Piers too. And don't worry: I'll be a great mother, believe me. Little junior, he'll have everything a kid can want. He deserves it. A rich little kid like that. And we'll be in charge of the money. It'll rub off on us, won't it, Dennis? We'll have everything we want, everything."

He said, again: "Wanda....."

She paid no attention. "I mean, it's his money, the kid's, but I'll be the guardian, won't I? So I'll have control of the money. And Dennis will adopt the kid. Unless.... Frank, we'll hire you as a lawyer...."

"No thanks," I said.

"Oh, you'll change your mind. If Dennis adopts him, here's the question: does the kid lose the money? I mean, he'll be Dennis's child legally. If that's the case, of course, we won't do the adoption thing. Can you check that out for us, Frank? I'll pay you, of course."

"Wanda," I said, "I can't check anything out for you. I can't take you on as a client. I represent other people, remember? People who want to fight your claims."

"Oh, don't be technical, Frank. You're the lawyer for the estate, so you're the lawyer for my little darling too. Anyway, it doesn't matter. There's a million lawyers in the world, we don't need you. Besides, we won't be around here. I think we'll live in Los Angeles. I'm from Australia, I don't like winters. Up here, I know there's no ice and snow, but I still think the weather stinks sometimes. In San Francisco, you could freeze to death, really, the cold fog, that sort of thing. We'll live in Beverly Hills. I'll hire nannies, too. We'll get a fancy stroller, and I'll go down the street with my little millionaire. That's what I'll do. You wait and see."

Dennis was looking more and more unhappy. I can't say I blamed him. She was indiscreet, to say the least.

"You know, Wanda," I said, "the family, they'll fight this every inch of the way. I'm not giving away any secrets. It's obvious that's what they're going to do. You're going to have to prove this is really the child of Piers Mobius. And how are you going to do that? DNA? The father's body, if this is his kid, is deep under the Pacific Ocean."

"You think we don't have proof? I have a witness, first of all."

"A witness?"

"Yes," she said. "Dennis was there. He saw the whole thing, blow by blow, if you know what I mean."

"You think people will believe him? Your boyfriend?"

"You say we're lying?" she said. "Don't deny it. Of course you are. But I told you: we'll swear on a stack of Bibles. You think I don't know what perjury is? We're telling the truth."

"And where did this take place? And when?"

"Why should I tell you? Oh, all right: in our favorite spot, the hotel in Brisbane."

Dennis glowered at her. She laughed and pinched him on the cheek. The baby had fallen asleep. She gathered him up and swept out of the room, with Dennis trailing behind.

She was a force of nature, I'll give her that. And who was that baby, really? The little newborn, wrapped in his little blanket? Was it a Mobius, after all? Or something else?

21

"She's lying, lying, lying. I just know it, Frank."

This was Doris, sitting in my office. I was not at all surprised by her reaction.

"She has no real proof," Doris said. "The boyfriend? That's a joke. He's lying too. Who would believe him? She thinks that if the two of them swear the baby is a Mobius, they'll get away with it. Well, they won't."

I wished I was that sure. Doris went on: "But what I really came to talk to you about, is something that simply flabbergasted me. Derek. My brother. He said he had something he wanted to share with me, he was sorry he hadn't done this before, and so on and so on, and he ended up showing me this supposed confession, Grampa's confession. I couldn't believe it. Everybody in that family is a wackjob. Every last Mobius except me. I must be a 100% Hayden. I said to Mother, was I adopted? I must have been adopted. She said, don't be ridiculous, why are you saying such a thing. I said, because I'm not insane. All of the Mobius people have a screw loose except me. She said, what about Derek? And I said, Mother, he's as bad as the rest of them. But she just laughed."

"Derek must have told you he showed me the confession."

"Yes, he told me that."

"OK," I said. "There's just the two of us here, Doris. Tell me what you think. Something about this confession thing, it just doesn't seem right to me either."

"Yes, I'm just as skeptical as you are," she said. "I wasn't close to my grandfather, neither of us was, but I did know him somewhat. What I'm going to say, it's going to sound terrifically disloyal."

"Disloyal?"

"To my brother. My only brother. But Frank, I need to talk to somebody. I've got to vent a little. Listen: Grampa never killed anybody. I know that. He was simply incapable of such a thing."

"You mean physically?"

"Well, yes, physically he *was* in bad shape. But more than that, psychologically. I can't picture it, I just can't. And his own brother! The fact is, he loved the guy. God knows why: filthy old miser. But Grampa always used to say that blood is thicker than water. And you have to remember, Grampa was a sour, lonely old man. No family really. You can't count us as family. Derek and I, sure, there was no sharp break; but it's not as if we saw him often. And, well, it just wasn't the same, I mean, his relationship with us. We had nothing in common, really. He and his brother, after all, they grew up together, they had a whole life together, if you know what I mean."

"So then why the confession? You don't think it's genuine?"

"Oh it's genuine, I'm pretty sure," she said. "No, it's something else. I think Grampa was trying to protect somebody. He knew he was old and dying, and he thought, I might as well take the blame."

"The blame? But for who?"

"That's the awful thing," she said. "That's what really bothers me. If he was protecting somebody, there's only one person who that could be: my brother."

"Derek?"

"Yes, Derek."

"You mean your *brother* killed old Mobius?"

She looked at me, closely. Doris was a formidable woman, I knew that already. Her voice was clear and steady. "I'm not making any accusations. Maybe it was self-defense. I just don't know the whole story. Do I think Derek is capable of killing somebody? No, I don't. But maybe he knows something. He was there. At the apartment that day. And I can't help thinking, our grandfather was trying to protect him. That's why he wrote that crazy confession."

I needed some time to digest this. The old man had confessed to the murder. As Doris said, it seemed improbable. But the alternative seemed almost equally improbable. Derek Mobius? My young, clean-cut client? A law student? Could he possibly have gone up the stairs and shot his uncle to death?

I just couldn't see it. And, if he was telling the truth, he never actually went *inside* the apartment. But if not Derek, then who? Was somebody else in the apartment? Fern Plotnick? Or Doris herself? I didn't dare ask her if she had an alibi.

If it was Derek, then at least the confession made sense. Give the document to Derek, and if the police ever start sniffing about, he could whip it out, and that puts an end to the investigation. And yet....

That evening, I sat in an easy chair, staring at a magazine, but I wasn't reading it. I was thinking about Rupert Mobius, his untimely death, and the whole colorful cast of characters. In my mind, I divided them into two groups: people I thought just might be capable of killing somebody and people who I thought couldn't possibly do such a thing. I know: you can't really be sure. Either way people can fool you. Still, in my mind, I made out my list.

People at least possibly able to kill somebody: here I put three strong and self-willed women, Wanda, Katerina, and... well, Doris, I guess. Of these three, Wanda was the most likely. She was a real she-devil and certainly dishonest, money-mad, and a born schemer.

Were there men who might possibly be killers? Nobody really—nobody very likely. I guess I couldn't rule out Gideon. Derek? Or perhaps the shadowy figure of the

Reverend Elijah Foster-Morrison? I hadn't had the pleasure yet of meeting him. And the dead grandfather? He, after all, had actually confessed. But he was old and sick....

Who do I rule out? Fern Plotnick? I just couldn't picture her doing anything so violent. Ms. Guthrie?

On Saturday, I had some work to do at the office; and Celia was off on a retreat with some of her colleagues. Actually, she dreaded the idea: "Five days a week is enough," she said; but still, she felt she had to go, so she went. In the afternoon, I drove into the city on an impulse. It was an overcast, dreary winter day. I drove to the building where the murder took place. I simply had to see something for myself. It was a big, ugly building. I found a parking spot about a block away.

Of course there was no doorman or anything like that. I walked in the front door, into a dirty hallway, the walls covered with graffiti. It looked as if dozens of people lived in the building; there was a whole flock of mailboxes and buzzers you could ring to alert somebody you were on your way. But there were no locked doors: anybody could walk in and go up the stairs, or use the rickety elevator. There was a utility room on the ground floor and another room with coin-operated washing machines and dryers.. I poked my head in. A young man, scrawny and pale, was doing his wash. He was wearing a white t-shirt, and was barefoot, with pierced ears and tattoos on his neck. He stared at me as he stuffed underwear into a washing machine. I closed the door quickly.

There was also a back entrance, leading into an alleyway where the garbage cans were located. The door to the alley was unlocked.

In other words, somebody could have been upstairs in Rupert Mobius' apartment on that fatal day; and that somebody could have shot Rupert, walked down the stairs, or even taken the elevator... and then out the back door, into the alley, then wherever. And it would be quite likely that nobody saw this man (or woman), or thought anything of it.

22

When I got to my office the next morning, I was very surprised to see Katerina Mobius in the corridor, obviously waiting for me.

Fortunately—or maybe I mean unfortunately—I had nobody scheduled for the morning, so I was free to talk to Katerina. I motioned her into my office.

"Cranshaw is parking the car," she said. "Parking is a nightmare here; it's almost as bad as San Francisco."

I said nothing. It was odd, to say the least, to have this kind of visit. She said, "I told my lawyer I was going to come and confront you, and he told me not to."

"I see how much you pay attention," I said. Maybe I shouldn't have shown her my annoyance, but it was hard not to.

"Oh, Frank, you lawyers! Everything so technical. And so timid. Our lawyer said, well, if you insist on going, I have to come with you. I said no, this is not for you. Trust me, I said. Of course he doesn't trust me. He wants everything done a certain way. But no, I don't believe in that kind of cat-and-mouse game."

I said nothing. Cranshaw appeared at that point, somewhat breathless. She asked him if he found a place to park. He had. "Two blocks away. I had to put in all my quarters and dimes. It's good for an hour and a few minutes. I'm out of change now."

"Maybe Frank has change," she said. "I suppose this is something he has to do for his clients." I was about to

138

tell her, no, I don't give my clients money for parking meters, but she went on to say: "Anyway, this won't take an hour, Cranshaw. Not even close. I'm going to say what I have to say; and then we'll leave. Maybe half an hour."

He said in a gloomy voice: "I wasted fifty cents."

She said to me: "Cranshaw is careful about money. But then he has to be. We have nothing, nothing: and our father was a millionaire. A millionaire! And the money, where is it going? To people he barely knew. That's part of it, and the rest is going to some creatures who were taking advantage of him, bloodsuckers, and he was old and sick and his mind was failing. It's the injustice of it all. You think we're in it for the money, but it's family, it's justice, that's why we're fighting for our rights."

Cranshaw nodded his head.

"We're contesting the will," she said, "you know that. Your clients... our lawyer tells us they can't get the money. It's blood money. It's murder money. You know that. Anyway, poor Father wasn't in his right mind, and this woman, this Plotnick person, and this phony reverend, they poisoned his mind. That's what they call undue influence, that's the term, my lawyer explained it to me. I wanted to make sure you understood that. We have the law on our side. He told us that."

"I'm sure you think so, Katerina," I said, "but that's not the way we see it. I don't think I should be talking to you, really. I do have to say, though, that your case is actually pretty weak. You seem to assume that your uncle killed your father. But we don't really know that. And nobody has been charged with the murder. You must know that."

"Oh come on! Simon did it. It's as plain as the nose on your face. The police thought so, and they have good evidence."

"Evidence?"

"They do. And you know what? Some of it is evidence *I* gave them. The day he died, I was at his building—you didn't know that, did you? Well, I was. I woke up that morning, and I decided, I have to try to reach out to my poor father. One last try. It hurt me, it was like a knife in my heart, the way my own father treated me, like some sort of Hitler. That's what I said to Cranshaw, I said, Cranshaw, we have to try. We're his flesh and blood. And we have to rescue him from those bloodsuckers. So, in the afternoon, I got in my car, and I drove to that awful place he was living."

"You actually went to see him? What did he say?"

"Nothing. I didn't see him. I didn't go up. To my dying day, I'll regret it." She wiped away a tear. Cranshaw reached over and patted her back.

"You didn't go in the building?"

"No, I didn't. Father could be, well, difficult. His mental condition.... When I got there, I called him on my cellphone from the car. It rang and rang, and then that Plotnick woman answered, and she said, who is this? And I hung up immediately, I wasn't going to talk to her. I thought, oh, I can't go up, she's there, I'll come back another time. But there wasn't going to be another time, the poor man was dead."

"So... you drove home?"

"Oh, no. Right then, I saw my uncle coming out of the building, and there was something about the way he was behaving that.... Well, it was just plain strange, suspicious, something like that."

"Suspicious?"

"Well, he kept looking around, as if he was afraid somebody would see him, and... trust me, I knew something was up. I thought, what's going on? He'd been there, in the apartment, and so was that Plotnick person. So I sat there in my car and I watched him. Oh yes—and this is important—he was carrying some sort of bundle, something wrapped in a paper bag. He walked to the corner and he got in a car. I decided to follow him. I had some sort of instinct: I'm a very intuitive person. And, because of the way he was acting... I thought, where is he going? What is this all about."

"So you followed him."

"I did. By the way, he wasn't driving the car. Somebody else was in the car, in the driver's seat. I didn't see who it was at first. Anyway, they drove across the city, and then they parked at a spot on the ocean side, where there's a steep cliff, and you can walk to the edge of the cliff. The other person got out of the car. I didn't recognize the man, but I know who it is now, because I've met him. It was my cousin, Derek."

"And then?"

"It was getting dark, and it was hard to see. I parked my car and I tried to make out exactly what this man was doing. He was carrying the bundle. I slid down in my car. I didn't want him to see me."

"And then?"

"He waited for a while. I think he wanted it to get totally dark. Then he went down the path. I didn't follow him of course. But he dumped the bundle in the ocean. I didn't see this, but I know it happened. When he came back, he didn't have the bundle anymore. He got back into the car and they drove off."

"Did you follow him again?"

"Well, I tried, but I lost him in rush hour traffic. It can be horrible in that part of town. So I gave that up."

"And then? Did you go back to your father's place?"

"Oh, if only! I wish I had... but by then I was late for an appointment. I was supposed to go to my hairdresser. His name is Henri. Nobody else can do my hair the way Henri does. But he's very temperamental: he can't *stand* it if you come the least bit late. And he had made a special appointment, I mean, seeing me so late in the day. So I just went on to Henri. He's in downtown Burlingame, and I knew the traffic would be simply awful. And when I think that all this time, my father was lying there dead, and that his own brother killed him, and that this creature, Plotnick, was there, and here I was sitting in a chair, and Henri was doing my hair and gossiping: oh, it's really so dreadful, I don't even like to think about it, but of course I can't get it out of my mind."

Another tear slid out of her eyes. "So you see," she said, "Uncle shot him, that's clear, and then he got rid of the gun. And that woman was involved, too. When we go to trial, I'll put Derek Mobius on the stand, and we'll win our case."

"You're sure it was Derek, driving."

"Oh, I'm sure. And I hired a private investigator, I've got the license plate number, and of course it was Derek. Now that I've actually seen him, I'm one hundred percent sure. And maybe we can dredge for the gun...."

"In the Pacific Ocean? Really, Katerina. And your uncle is dead. Even if he wasn't," I said, "and they put him on trial, you couldn't get a conviction. Not on that kind of evidence. And that bundle, or paper bag, or whatever it was: you never actually saw what was in it, now did you? It could be anything."

"Don't be ridiculous. What else was in the bundle? My father's laundry? Be serious. But maybe that Fern person killed him, and my uncle was trying to cover up, to protect her. Even so, he'd be an accomplice, wouldn't he?"

"But why on earth would he protect Fern Plotnick? He hardly knew her."

"Oh, how should I know? Maybe they had a deal to split up my poor father's money. They could be in it together. But really, I don't think she did it. My uncle did. And I think we could convince a court. My lawyer told me, it can be done. O. J. Simpson...."

"O. J. Simpson?"

"That stupid jury let him go. But then they sued him—the family sued him—and they won. That's what my lawyer told me. We could do the same."

I had no wish to argue points of law with Katerina Mobius. She went on for a while, explaining how she had a strong case, that she had gone to the police with her information, and that our case was hopeless, and so on.

I had a different idea. I think her lawyer, who was nobody's fool, had told her the opposite: that her case was weak, and that it would be better to settle out of court. She was on a reconnaissance mission. Of course, it was folly on her part, but then Katerina was a very foolish woman. Settlement was a real possibility, but it would take careful negotiation and it should have been left to the lawyers. In the end, Katerina left, with Cranshaw trailing behind. I wonder if they got their money's worth at the parking meter.

23

Everybody involved in this sordid affair seemed to be using private investigators. Well, not everybody; but a fair number of people whose last name was Mobius. Among them of course was Doris. I asked her how the investigation was coming. She said she had learned all sorts of interesting things. And she invited me over to her condo for dinner. "Your wife, too, of course." But Celia refused to go. "I can't stand business dinners, and that's what this is," she said. "Tell her I have a headache."

"I'm making pasta," Doris said. "Derek and my mother are coming at 7:30, but, Frank, I want you to come at 7:00. Then we can talk."

Doris' condo was small but neat, everything in good taste. She offered me a drink, which I refused. The dinner was all ready, she said, she just needed to heat things for a few minutes.

She was a very efficient woman. That was obvious. And a woman with strong opinions.

"Frank," she said, sitting down across from me, in her living room. We were nibbling on cheese and crackers. "That woman's nerve, it's absolutely appalling."

"Which woman are you talking about? Katerina, or Wanda?"

"Well, I suppose they're both appalling," she said. "Not to mention this Plotnick creature. But Wanda is the most appalling. Katerina is irritating, but she's not a criminal. Anyway, Wanda had the nerve to call me and talk about the estate and her baby's share and all that rubbish. And shouldn't we be friends since we're all family, and so on. As if she gave a crap about family. All she cares about is money. I lost my temper with her. I said, listen, you and your little bastard won't inherit a penny if I have anything to say about it. It's not my father's kid, and that's that. You're lying through your teeth, but you won't get away with it. "

"And what did she say?"

"Oh, we'll see about that, or something along those lines. I mean, the colossal gall! Actually, I feel sorry for the kid. What kind of a mother is that, and God knows who the father is. She'll probably give the kid away, give it up for adoption as soon as this is over. Because it will be over. And we'll have the last laugh."

"How's that, Doris?"

"She thinks we don't have DNA. She thinks we can't prove the kid isn't what we say it is. I understand her plan. She'll swear and swear and swear that it's a Mobius child; and since we won't be able to prove it isn't, she'll either get a share or force us to pay her off with big money. But we can foil that nasty little plan. We can *prove* the child doesn't belong to our family."

"You can prove it, Doris?"

"With DNA."

"Fantastic. But... how? The body is gone, isn't it?"

"Oh yes, the body is gone. But our investigators in Australia, they've done a terrific job: they found something really interesting. It seems that my father at one time had a mole removed from his left cheek at a hospital in Brisbane. They were worried that it was possibly cancerous. Anyway, the physician who removed it, a Dr. Ludwig, I don't remember his first name, something foreign-sounding, anyway, he kept the mole."

"Why on earth would he do that, Doris? Is that the usual practice? I once had a mole removed. I don't like to think my dermatologist just filed it away in a drawer. I assume it went in the garbage." I hated to think there were fragments of my body stashed away in medical offices.

"Well," she said, "this doctor did keep the mole, he really did. It's because father *asked* him to. We told you he was obsessed with this stuff, life after death, and I don't mean up in heaven, he wasn't the least bit religious, no, he meant life after death right here on earth. He was into cryogenics: getting frozen so that science could revive him later on. He made all those arrangements, apparently. Well, naturally he couldn't know that he would end up at the bottom of the Pacific Ocean, but he did worry about whether or not there would *be* a body, or whether it would be gone for one reason or another. That's what he told Dr. Ludwig. And he made Dr. Ludwig promise to keep the mole, so that, if worst came to worst.... Well, when we told him about this baby, this absurd idea, that Piers Mobius was supposedly the father of this child born after his death, well, he said, yes, if we could produce something from the baby, he could do whatever it is that they do to figure out whether or not the kid really is the child of Piers Mobius. So that's the situation."

"Amazing!" I said. "Does Wanda know about this?"

"Not yet. And if the mole isn't enough, believe it or not, there's a toenail. An ingrown toenail. The podiatrist's name is Dr. Gunnar Chung. Same story in general. Our father wanted the nail preserved, or at least the part at the base that might contain useful DNA. Dr. Chung still has it. Father wanted some backup, in the form of items that carried his DNA. Of course, this would not be as good as defrosting a whole body, you'd have to clone a whole new person from these cells. Still, he told the doctors this was better than nothing, and he made them promise not to throw the stuff away."

"Amazing," I said again. It *was* consistent with what Wanda had said about Mobius. Yet probably she knew nothing about the mole and the toenail. All this made her sperm story a bit more credible. I mentioned this to

Doris. She shrugged it off. She felt utterly confident. "I haven't broken the news to her yet," she said. "About the mole and the toenail. She won't be happy. It'll be the end of her precious little scheme."

"Let me know what happens," I said. At that point Derek and their mother arrived. We stayed off the subject of murder, estates, toenails, and related matters. The food, by the way, was excellent. But the conversation dragged, and I left as early as I could.

A few days later, Doris called me. Agitated. She'd just talked to Wanda some more about the baby. "To tell the truth, I said to her, I feel sorry for the kid. She laughed and said, don't feel sorry. Little Piers has a very bright future. Very, very bright. I felt like strangling her."

"Did you tell her... about the mole and the toenail?"

"I told her we knew she was lying and that we were in a position to prove it."

She said, "Oh, really? And how is that? I said, never mind. You just wait and see. Then she said to me, what's your home address? And when I asked her what for, she said oh, we're sending out a few birth announcements, and we're going to send you one. This is your baby brother, after all. I slammed down the phone, I couldn't take it anymore."

"How are you going to arrange for the DNA testing? You've got to get a sample or something from this baby."

"Don't worry. I'll manage," she said.

And, as you shall see, she did.

24

The next few days, I worked hard—but not on anything to do with the estates of Rupert and Simon Mobius. They were, in any event, a hopeless mess. I got tired just thinking about these matters.

I thought, why couldn't they be like the estate of a dream client: Martha Wilson Trimble. I was preparing to do the last things I needed to do, to wind up this estate—distributing the assets, closing it out, discharging the executor. Martha Wilson Trimble had been a wealthy widow. She was 75 years old, and lived in a very expensive condominium in Palo Alto. The estate consisted of a rich portfolio of stocks and bonds, the condo itself, and some jewelry and odds and ends. Martha had once owned a Mercedes but she gave it up when her eyesight deteriorated: she used cabs instead.

I inherited Martha from her late husband, who made his money in real estate, but sold it all just before he died. Martha was cranky and difficult, but only when she was alive. Dead, she was a dream come true. She had no children. She left her entire estate to the Presbyterian Church. She had an accountant in Los Gatos who prepared her tax returns and kept track of all her financial matters. She named him executor. (I had drafted the will.) There were no problems, no estate tax issues, no scheming heirs. Everything was in apple-pie order. There was practically no work to be done. The accountant was fussy and pedantic, but he was the ideal executor; he did everything right.

Martha died, I should add, in the nick of time. Both my daughters needed expensive orthodontist work. I say "needed," but the "need" was a subject of intense discussion. Celia said: "There's something wrong with their bite. It has to be fixed." I saw nothing wrong with their bite. When I was young, nobody worried about their bite. I said so.

"Times have changed," Celia said.

I balked at the horrendous expense. Then Martha died. The issue was closed. Martha's sudden heart attack while she was vacationing in Phoenix on her way to the Grand Canyon with a tour group, settled the issue. The fees were going to be substantial. My daughters' teeth were destined to be the envy of the neighborhood.

That was the late Martha Trimble. Simon Mobius, of course, was another story altogether.

"We're going to have to reach some sort of settlement," Gideon said to me, on the phone, in a gloomy voice. "That's the only way."

I had to agree.

But it takes two to tango, and the parties involved have to *want* to come to an agreement. This means compromise. Derek and Doris would have come around, I think, despite their utter loathing for everybody else involved. But Katerina and Cranshaw turned suddenly quite adamant. They said—or rather Katerina said—they would fight to the death over "poor Daddy's estate." "Our dear father," she said, "he was misled, he was cheated, and now he's gone. We want justice to be done. That's it. Justice."

Cranshaw was no doubt nodding in the background.

"It's not the money," she said. Of course nobody believed her. They had their own lawyer now, this fellow Arpad, a slick operator apparently—and they had now actually filed papers, begun a lawsuit; and were threatening a genuine knock-down, drag-out will contest.

Then there was another party to consider as well: Fern Plotnick. Persuading her to cooperate was also a difficult task. And she, after all, had been named executor of the estate of Rupert Mobius.

Arpad, after filing in court, invited all the concerned parties to a meeting which he called a "settlement discussion" (which of course confirmed our feeling that the lawsuit was a tactic, and that "poor Daddy's estate" would be sold down the river, provided Gideon and company were willing to pay enough). It was supposed to be "very informal, just preliminary discussions." We all gathered at the appointed time in Gideon's plush conference room: Katerina and Cranshaw, Doris and Derek, and myself. "Where's Arpad?" I asked.

"I told him not to come," Katerina said. "He made a fuss, but he had to agree."

Gideon was totally disgusted. "I fail to see the point...."

Of course Gideon was entirely right to be disgusted. Without the lawyer for Katerina and Cranshaw, it was hard to see how we could make any progress. But Katerina had a mind of her own. "I wanted this to be mostly family," she said. "A family discussion. We're all family, aren't we?"

I looked at Gideon, and he looked at me. *We* certainly weren't family. "And it would be *so* much better without any of the lawyers," Katerina said. But Doris insisted that we stay. She at least had some sense. She said: "Katerina, yes, we're all related. That's true. But we don't know you, you don't know us. So if you're talking about some sort of relationship, let's be honest: we don't have one. As far as I'm concerned, you're complete strangers; and that's why I'd like this to be business-like. I want Frank to stay. And you too, Gideon."

"OK, if you insist," Katerina said. "But I hope we can avoid conflict. Arpad says nobody wins if there's conflict."

I said, "Katerina, nobody likes conflict. But you're the

source of the conflict. You've filed a lawsuit. You're claiming your father wasn't competent mentally, you're accusing Ms. Plotnick of undue influence, and you're also saying my clients' grandfather killed his brother. You're trying to get the police involved again. Anyway, if you win your lawsuit, then you and your brother get everything and my clients get nothing. So, I'm afraid, unless we can reach some sort of agreement—well, frankly, conflict is the name of the game."

"Our poor daddy! His troubles even go past the grave," she said. I fully expected tears, which she seemed able to turn on and off at will. "He really wasn't himself. You know that as well as we do...."

"I never met him," I said. "He seemed able to handle his money, make investments, live a life."

"But what about this perfectly absurd foundation? Isn't that the work of this Plotnick woman, and that scheming Reverend? Of course it is. Surely you can go along with us on that one. It doesn't concern your clients at all, as far as I can see."

I was about to comment on this when Ms. Guthrie came into the room and said that there were two people outside who were insisting on seeing Gideon. "That's out of the question, Ms. Guthrie; as you can see, I'm in conference. And I didn't have anybody scheduled."

"I told them that. It's Fern Plotnick, and some man."

"Tell them I'm busy, I can't possibly see them." But this was useless. Before Ms. Guthrie could even leave the room, Fern Plotnick appeared in the doorway. Her gray hair was more disheveled than ever. She was wearing a long skirt and sandals. She was arm in arm with a man in his 40's. He was tall, with very dark hair and somewhat oily skin. He had a neatly trimmed goatee, and he was wearing a dark suit, with a clerical collar.

I felt a small, distant burst of pity for Gideon. No doubt he had difficult clients—we all do—but Fern Plotnick was way beyond difficult. And his position was touchy. He was supposed to represent the estate of Rupert Mobius: he was the attorney for the estate and for the executor and thus for Fern Plotnick as well. He had the duty, too, to defend the provisions of the will, including the foundation, which of course he found quite absurd.

"Ms. Plotnick," he said. "Really. We are having a meeting here and...." He never finished the sentence. He realized, of course, that Fern Plotnick should have been invited. Naturally, nobody wanted her. "Who is this gentleman?"

The man extended his hand to Gideon. "I'm the Reverend Elijah Foster-Morrison. Ms. Plotnick is one of my flock."

"I really have to ask you to go," Gideon said. "This is a closed meeting. Please, Ms. Plotnick."

She paid no attention to him. She stared at everyone in the room. "I've heard from Rupert," she said. "I've had messages from him."

Dead silence in the room.

"I warned him," she said. "He defied the spirit world. There were pictures of the spirits in the photo album. That's why it was taken away. And now Rupert is one of the spirits himself."

The Reverend nodded his head in agreement. "Ms. Plotnick is a very spiritual person," he said. "I take her comments most seriously."

We were all dumbfounded: it appeared that she was completely out of her mind, and that this supposed Reverend was egging her on. The biggest burden was going to fall on Gideon: could he have her removed as executor and trustee?

"Ms. Plotnick," he said. "I'm sure the, uh, spirits are extremely active, and we welcome your comments. But we are discussing legal matters here."

Katerina was much less reticent. "Fern," she said. "I might as well tell you. My brother and I are contesting this supposed foundation. And the whole will, for that matter. Our belief is that this foundation is illegal. And that my poor father was... somewhat unbalanced and in no position to make out *any* sort of will. And we will prove that in court."

Fern Plotnick seemed not to hear a word of this. "The spirits can do anything. They are everywhere, even in this room. You can feel their presence."

This was too much for Derek, "This woman is bonkers," he said, in a whisper, and then, in a louder voice, "why don't we just adjourn this meeting, and get together some other time?"

The Reverend chimed in, with a booming and somewhat gaseous voice: "Do I understand you to say that you are challenging the foundation that my late friend wanted to establish? Can that be true?"

"*They* are challenging it," Derek said, pointing to Katerina and Cranshaw.

"I object very strongly," he said. "My late friend was very much concerned with these issues of the spirit, and do not all of us feel sometimes in the presence of a higher power? I cannot think of a better, more noble use of the money."

This was too much for Derek. "Oh, come off it. This is some kind of crazy cult, and if a court strikes it down, I say more power to them."

"Do you accept the Holy Bible?" he asked, frowning at Derek.

"None of your business," he said.

The Reverend went on: "The Bible tells us all about the spirits. Good spirits, and evil spirits. It's all in the Bible: Satan, Book of Job, angels, cherubim and seraphim. The heavenly host."

"Oh, come on," Derek said. "The whole thing is a fairy tale from start to finish. Adam and Eve and all that, Noah's Ark. I mean, really."

The Reverend waggled his finger and fixed his beady eyes on Derek. "Noah's Ark? It happened. The destruction of the world because of sin and vice. And it can happen again. The world is going to be judged. There's going to be a new flood. The glaciers are melting all over the Arctic. The waters are rising, rising. It's beginning to happen."

"And are we supposed to build an ark?" Derek said, with a sneer.

"A spiritual ark, yes. In Biblical times they built a physical ark. But the world is different now."

"Oh, really now," Derek said. "Do you actually believe that story about Noah and the Ark? I mean, the whole thing is completely ridiculous. Ridiculous! Did you know there are 35,000 species of mammals? That's a lot of mammals. If they came in pairs, that makes 70,000 animals, and some of them are huge, like elephants. How could they all fit on the boat? Not to mention amphibians, reptiles, and birds...."

"The birds could fly," said the Reverend.

"Well, most of them, but not the ostriches. Anyway, that's neither here nor there. And what did everybody eat? On the ark, I mean. If there were two tigers, they'd make short work of the deer on board, and if you kept the tigers away from the deer, they'd starve to death. And what about things like kangaroos? Or rabbits, or whatever? Where would they get the grass?"

The Reverend smiled mysteriously. "God can do anything."

"That's a cop-out," Derek said.

Fern had been listening, and seemed to be getting more and more agitated. Now she put in her two cents. She said, "I believe in the Bible. There could have been a miracle. Maybe all the animals, they shrank, they were little tiny things so he could get them all on the boat."

"And the food?"

"Some kind of manna, something that came from heaven...."

The Reverend slammed his fist on the glass coffee table, and said, in a loud voice, "We are not here to make arguments. We are here to carry out the wishes of the deceased. Noble wishes, I might add."

Gideon, however, had had enough. "This meeting is adjourned," he said, "I have an important appointment in court. Ms. Guthrie will show you all out." Which she did.

25

I was, of course, not a party to the will contest, though I paid close attention to it. Katerina and Cranshaw—well, really Katerina—and their lawyer were pursuing their attack on the will quite aggressively. The basic claim was that the old man had been unhinged, unable mentally to execute a valid will.

This attack on what we lawyers call "testamentary capacity" is usually a fairly desperate ploy. I assume that Arpad was a competent attorney and knew this as well as we did. I felt sure he was simply angling for the best possible settlement. He and his clients were basically grasping at straws. The old man was eccentric, annoying, unhygienic, yes; but insane? Insane enough so that he was not legally entitled to execute a will? Legally speaking, that's a pretty tall order. But it does work, once in a while. Old Rupert had cut off his children: that was a help. Courts don't like that kind of thing. It makes the will "unnatural." That's the legal term. I suppose any judge who actually knew Katerina and Cranshaw might think Rupert's will was a bit less unnatural than would normally be the case.

Much of the testimony was in the form of depositions, and Gideon kept me in the picture, sending me transcripts regularly. I won't bore you with all the testimony, but I'll give you a taste of it. This is from the deposition of a woman named Myrtle Applebaum. Two years or so before his death, Rupert had a very serious illness of some sort, hepatitis I think: he was hospitalized and then sent home to convalesce. Katerina hired a woman to take care of him over Rupert's strenuous objections. Ms. Applebaum weighed 300 pounds, was about 50 years old, and was both bossy and opinionated. She and Rupert fought like cats and dogs, and he finally fired her in a burst of anger. She moved to Wichita, Kansas, where the deposition was taken. After Rupert, she considered giving up the caregiver business altogether, but then she was hired to take care of a wealthy real estate mogul, who was 90 years old and seriously demented. It was at times not the most pleasant job in the world; the man was extremely feeble and rarely opened his mouth, but he was (for Myrtle) quite easy to handle.

Myrtle Applebaum obviously hated Rupert, and was very bitter about the way he treated her. She was only too glad to describe him as a lunatic. But her actual evidence was hardly overwhelming.

"I remember he was eating a piece of carrot cake. He used his fingers, not a fork, and he was picking out the raisins. He'd look at each individual raisin, and make some kind of noise...."

"Q: A noise?"

"A: Yes, a noise. I can't describe it any better. Like a grunt. Sometimes like a squeak, you know, squeaky like. I'd say, don't do that. Well, he paid no attention to me, unless he was yelling. Anyway, he'd pick out this raisin, and then he'd throw it away. Sometimes he would just throw it on the floor. I said Mr. Mobius, who do you expect to pick up that raisin? I'm not a housemaid. He didn't care."

"Q: You said he was always dirty...."

"A: Well, I had to wash him, at first. But then he was strong enough to do it himself. But he didn't. And he never changed his underwear. He wore the same underwear, day after day, week after week. I tried my best to get him to do something about this. I said, Mr. Mobius, this is disgusting, it smells, but he laughed in my face. I used to take things to the laundromat. It wasn't my job, but I did it anyway. And I'd bring back clean underwear. He wouldn't wear it. I like the dirty ones, he said. Big holes in them, too, it was disgusting."

"Q: In what other ways did you find his behavior, well, strange?"

Gideon objected to this question, and a long argument followed. Gideon, of course, was just doing his duty. Secretly, I suppose, he probably thought Rupert Mobius was at least mildly unhinged. But his only hope of a fee was to uphold the will. If Katerina and Cranshaw succeeded in their lawsuit, as I think I explained, the will would be thrown out. There wasn't any other will, and that would make Gideon an "intestate." Katerina and Cranshaw would get everything as the closest relatives; Arpad would get a juicy fee; and Gideon would be out of the picture.

Gideon called me from time to time, and we discussed the case. He was positive (as I was) that Katerina and Cranshaw would call off their lawsuit, if they were offered enough money. It was tempting to play hardball, he said, because he was convinced the Mobius children would lose. "All this nonsense about raisins and underwear: that doesn't mean a thing. I have brokers and bankers, and all of them can testify the old man was shrewd and cunning, that he understood the stock market perfectly—so how could he be insane?" Still, he recognized that, in any lawsuit, there was always a risk. And Gideon was not a man who liked risks.

One thing surprising about this and other depositions, recording the testimony of witnesses that Rupert's children dredged up: nothing was said about the spirits or about Fern Plotnick. She was apparently a fairly recent acquisition. No doubt if the case proceeded, the Mobius children would certainly bring in alleged hallucinations and the "undue influence" which they claimed Fern Plotnick exerted—aided and abetted in this regard by the so-called Reverend.

For my part, I also wished they would stop urging the police to reopen the murder case. That was a matter that concerned me deeply. Pinning the murder on Simon Mobius could be a real blow to *my* clients.

I had always thought some sort of settlement was likely. But the road to get there was going to be rocky. Katerina—who persisted in bypassing her own lawyer—was quite explicit: in a conversation with Gideon she told him, "No sir, we are not going to settle. It's a matter of principle. We want justice to be done. My poor father: no, we have to avenge his death. The dear old man, helpless, with that awful woman taking advantage of him, poisoning his mind. To think of him slaughtered in his own home, and by his brother. No, Mr. Grambling, we are not for sale."

But when Gideon dealt with Arpad, he heard another story. Arpad was much more sensible. He understood that the lawsuit was a long shot. He said to Gideon quietly: "Katerina, well, she's difficult; but I wouldn't take these things too literally. Let me talk to her. She's the only one that counts. The brother is irrelevant. He does what she says. I think she'll come around."

Gideon of course tried to persuade him to drop the lawsuit.

"Well, that's premature," Arpad told him, in one of their phone conversations. "And, yes, I do think we have a strong case, a very strong case. No, I am confident we'd win in court. But, naturally it would be better to come to some friendly agreement. Avoid all the costs and delays."

This was surely a bluff. He was trying to raise the price of the settlement: that was pretty clear to me. Both sides were now playing chicken.

Then there was the issue of Wanda Skadden. And that came suddenly to a boil.

26

At this point, nothing about this whole mess seemed clear. But I was thinking and thinking. All I had to go on were hunches. Still, hunches were proliferating. They centered on Wanda Skadden. I felt the more we knew about her, the better. I didn't at this time see the connection, if there was one, between Wanda and the murder of Rupert Mobius. But this brazen idea of passing off a baby as the child of Piers Mobius....

I said to Doris, "I'd like you to do something you maybe don't want to do. I'd like you to go see Wanda...."

"Frank: do I have to?"

"Listen to me: I'd like you to go and say to her, you want to see the baby, she says it's your little brother, and you'll say you don't think so, but you want to see for yourself, see if there's a resemblance, make up any old story. Take a good camera. Tell Wanda the baby is so cute and so on, and you want to take pictures of the baby, and then say you'd like pictures of mother and child. Get a good photo of Wanda. I think it's important. And somehow get her out of the room, and get a sample of the baby's DNA."

"How do you do that, Frank?"

"I think it's something to do with a cheek swab. Look it up, Doris. Anyway, that's terribly important. Then we can check it against the mole and the toenail. I mean, there are experts on this stuff. We can get a definitive answer. And if the baby's a fake, which we believe, that will help us get rid of Wanda Skadden once and for all."

Doris saw the point. The photographs were going to be very important. She was launching another and much more extensive investigation of Wanda Skadden, in Australia, and in the United States. "It's going to cost a lot of money," she said. "But it could be worth it."

Doris made the visit and she got the photographs. She also got the DNA sample. But the visit had another, perhaps surprising, result: she fell in love with the baby. "Frank," she said, "honestly, it's the cutest little thing. Little fat toes and thighs, I could squeeze the toes all day. I'm just so sorry it's stuck with that mother. I mean, no father at all, really, just that vicious, crooked psychopath of a mother. It's a crying shame."

"Psychopath? That's a little strong, Doris."

"Maybe. I don't know. But the baby, it's just plain adorable. I don't care whether it's my little baby brother or not. Did you know, Frank, I had a miscarriage once? I was married for a while, and the guy was a jerk, a loser, but never mind. I got pregnant, but I lost the baby. I guess that ever since... you see my point, though. I had this maternal thing, it swept all over me, I felt like crying. Holding the little thing in my arms. *She* obviously doesn't care for it at all. I mean that."

I steered the subject back to the precious DNA. "Now all we have to do is compare it with the mole," she said, "and we'll have the definitive proof."

And indeed it was definitive proof. The necessary procedures were followed; the tests were run; and the results were announced.

I won't bore you with scientific details. The news was a bombshell, delivered in cold, scientific language. While there was always a possibility of error in any human endeavor, the results were pretty much conclusive.

Wanda's baby was indeed the child of the late Piers Mobius.

27

As you can imagine, the news made quite a stir in the Mobius household—and in Wanda's, for that matter. Wanda, as soon as she heard the news, called me on the phone. She sounded... triumphant. "I told you so. You people, you thought I was lying. Well, I have the last laugh. My baby is going to be rich! How soon can we get some of that money? I want him to have the very best of care."

I had to dampen her enthusiasm a bit: handing over any sort of cash at this time was out of the question. And I reminded her that the money, if there was going to be any, would not be hers: it would belong to the baby and administered by the guardian.

"Well, I'm the guardian," she said. "I'm the mother."

I pointed out that there would have to be certain procedures.

"You lawyers!" she said, and hung up.

The conversation with Doris and Derek had a different tone. They were sitting in my office. Derek looked particularly glum. I said: "I know you're surprised, and it's a bitter pill to swallow. I'm not at all sure that this baby can inherit. It's a new situation, this business of having children after you're dead. The courts are just now wrestling with this. I mean, it's not the usual situation, to put it mildly. But remember, even if this baby *can* inherit, there's still going to be plenty of money for the two of you. That is, if we can fend off the lawsuit."

"But it's galling," Derek said. "That a creature like that woman can get her hands on a pile of money.... I mean, did our father really want this to happen? Did he want to become a father after he was dead? I don't think so."

"Derek, we have no idea what our father would want to happen. We never knew him," Doris said. "I'm trying to be philosophical. And this is our flesh and blood, after all. Think of the baby. It's not the baby's fault, now, is it? I know it's hard to deal with that awful woman. But I suppose we have to."

"Dodo," he said, "I wish you wouldn't rattle on about the baby."

She said: "Don't be so cold-blooded. You guys are all alike! After all, it *is* our brother—half-brother I suppose, but that doesn't matter. It's our own flesh and blood."

"I guess," he said, grudgingly.

She said to me: "The first time I mentioned my feelings about the baby, Derek absolutely laughed at me...."

"I did not!" he said.

"Oh, you did, Derek. You just don't care. I mean, you're as good as gold, and I love you, but when you get right down to it, you're a guy. And guys don't have any feelings for babies. I do. Maybe it's hormones, I don't know what. Frank, I told you about the miscarriage.... I really wish I had children. I love babies. Maybe someday I'll have children, if Mr. Right will only come along. Meanwhile, Frank, I'm going to ask you a serious question: do you think it's possible—I'm just asking—do you think I could maybe get custody of this baby?"

"You mean take it away from its mother?"

"I guess that is what I mean."

"That would be awfully tough, Doris. Legally, that's really hard to do. The mother has rights. So long as she isn't a criminal, or a drug addict...."

"A criminal," she said. "I see." Then she was silent. But I could read her mind. This was yet another motive for trying to dig up dirt about Wanda. If she found enough stuff, maybe she could get the child away from Wanda.

Derek, I could see, was far less enthusiastic. In Doris, however, I sensed a grim resolve.

When they left, I sat in my chair thinking. I too had been stunned by the news—by the DNA evidence. I had assumed, I guess, that Wanda was lying, that she was trying to extort money from the estate—that we would find a way to prove that she was a fraud.

On the other hand, the news made a certain amount of sense. I remembered some of the other odd things we knew about Piers Mobius. He was clearly obsessed with the idea of life after death—not in the religious sense, but quite literally. He wanted to freeze his body, after all, and he had the mole preserved. So it was not unreasonable to imagine that he would want his precious bodily fluids preserved. Not to make babies, but more likely to clone himself and come back from the dead.

I was not the only one to have this thesis. Fern Plotnick did, too, in a way. A crazy way, to be sure. She went to see the baby and gushed all over it (I heard this from Gideon, who found the whole matter disgusting). In fact, she told Wanda, and then Gideon: "This baby, it's Piers Mobius himself. He's come back. His soul is in this baby. It's made the journey back from the spirit world. I absolutely know that's true."

Nothing Fern Plotnick might say could surprise me anymore. I felt like asking Fern: and when exactly did this soul enter the picture? And how? I assume she knows about sperm and eggs and the rest of that biological business. Somehow these souls, floating around God knows where, are able to insinuate themselves into babies.

Who knows? Millions of people in the world believe in reincarnation. There's the Dalai Lama, for example, and he has all these devoted followers, even in the West. He comes to college campuses and he's greeted like a rock star.

I found myself spending a lot of time, mostly at night, thinking and thinking about this whole affair. Of course, the murder of Rupert Mobius was, in a way, none of my business and I had no forensic laboratories and no capacity to investigate. I had no way to ask people questions, interview suspects, nose around, or do any of the things the police could do. I also wondered whether I had enough of the "little gray cells" which gave Hercule Poirot the edge in solving crimes. But sometimes common sense can do the trick. Somehow, the DNA bombshell had to matter.... I felt myself groping toward something concrete, something still unformed. But growing.

28

A few days later, I went to see Wanda Skadden. You may well ask, why? Was it even proper? She had interests totally adverse to my clients. I should have dealt with her, if at all, only through her lawyer, if she had one by now. But I went out of sheer curiosity. And I felt there were some questions only she could answer. Any lawyer, of course, would tell her to keep quiet. I felt Wanda, in person, was not the type to keep quiet about anything.

She had moved into a rather shoddy apartment in Mountain View. It was in one of those sad little complexes that sprang up like mushrooms after the second World War. The peninsula has dozens of billionaires, and the whole area shrieks money; but there are also thousands of waiters, file clerks, cleaning ladies, and the like, and they all have to live somewhere. Some of them commute vast distances; others live in dreary apartments, made out of stucco and badly showing their age. That was the sort of complex that was now the home of Wanda Skadden and little Piers.

I had business with a client in Mountain View, and that gave me an excuse to be in the neighborhood. As I recall, it was a Thursday afternoon.

There was a note on Wanda's door. "Please do not ring doorbell." I dutifully knocked. At first nothing happened. I knocked again. The door opened a crack, and then wider. It was Wanda. She was wearing a kind of housedress, and her hair was a mess. There were bags

166

under her eyes.

"Oh, it's you," she said. "Couldn't imagine who'd be knocking. Well, come on in."

She led me into a small, dark living room. The furniture was late Salvation Army. She was reading my mind. "I rented it furnished," she said. "The stuff here, it's junk."

She cleared a pile of newspapers off a hideous sofa upholstered with some sort of nubby fabric, and motioned to me to sit down. "Thank God, the kid is asleep," she said. "Finally. I thought I would go out of my mind. Nobody ever warned me how much they yammer and scream. Maybe he has colic. I don't know what that is, to be honest. But I can't get him to stop crying sometimes... well, what the hell."

"Sorry you're having a problem," I said, lamely.

"A problem? I'll say. Listen, you think it's a picnic? The kid cries half the night, I'm not getting my beauty sleep. And diapers.... It's disgusting. I wish I had the money right now, money for a nanny. Boy, I just can't wait."

"Well, doesn't Dennis help out? I mean, I know he can't breast-feed...."

"You think I'm breast-feeding? No way. I quit that crap. The doctor talked to me about it, how it's so healthy and all. I said to her, do I look like a cow? The kid gets a bottle, he gets formula, it was good enough for me, probably. He's not going to die because I don't let him get near my nipples. I don't buy that propaganda—breast-feeding, mother nature. Mother nature can shove it, as far as I'm concerned."

"Well, then Dennis can give the kid a bottle, give you some relief."

"Are you kidding? Dennis? No way. He's not even around these days. Dennis, he's not the baby type. He's like a lot of men, they don't mind *making* babies, but that's about as far as it goes. Taking care of them, that's not their line at all. No, Dennis isn't in the picture. Not now, at any rate."

"He's... he's gone? He's not here?"

"That's what I said. He's not here. Let's say he's on a business trip".

"A business trip? What sort of business?"

"*His* business, Frank, not yours. OK? Let's leave it at that."

"And... is he coming back?"

"That's also none of your business."

We were off to a bad start. I tried asking her some different questions: like, when did she leave Australia. I had a feeling—well, more than feeling—that it was important to have an exact timeline of Wanda Skadden's activities. She didn't know, I hope, that Doris had launched a major investigation of her past. "You want the date? What for?"

I had trouble answering this question. And Wanda simply refused to answer. "What difference does it make?"

By now, she was openly hostile. In short, the visit was not a success. Wanda refused to answer any further questions; and, to make matters worse, the baby woke up and started screaming, which positively enraged its mother. She grabbed a bottle and a pacifier and stormed out of the living room. I beat an ignominious retreat. I had no inclination to stay around and watch this example of selfless motherhood. I was afraid that the baby might need a diaper change and that Wanda might enlist me in this enterprise. I had had my share of diapers, years before, and had no real desire to revive these long-lost skills. Maybe changing a diaper is like riding a bicycle: you never really lose the ability. But I wasn't about to test this hypothesis.

29

Nothing much happened for the next few days, except that Doris called me, not once, but twice, about the issue of custody.

"Really, Doris," I said, "there's nothing we can do. At the moment."

"She's not a fit mother, Frank. She's a horrible mother. I've been there again...."

"Why, Doris?"

"To see the baby. I love that baby, Frank. I really do. And to think, of him, living with that monster, and no father, and she doesn't care at all for the poor little thing."

I told her again how reluctant the courts were: they didn't like to wrench children away from parents unless the parents had done something truly awful.

"But she *has*. The woman is a criminal."

I thought this was somewhat exaggerated, but it turned out to be true. Doris called again, quite breathless. She was beginning to get further reports from Australia, and she was terrifically excited. The reports were supplemented with reports from the San Francisco area, as well. She wanted me to see the reports and she and Derek came to my office to hand me copies.

It was pretty startling reading. Wanda in fact was wanted on various charges in Australia, mostly fraud; and there was a movement to try to extradite her. The investigators had turned up information about the sperm donor scam and various other scams. Armed with the photographs, they traced her most recently to Brisbane, where they found that she had registered in a luxury hotel under an assumed name, Mrs. Felicity Frasco, with a man who called himself Earl Frasco. They stayed about three weeks, and then left in the middle of the night without bothering, of course, to pay their bill. They had presented a credit card when they registered. It was apparently valid, but then they canceled the card without telling the hotel, so that when they decamped, the hotel was left holding the bag.

The photos had turned out to be quite useful. They made it easy to identify this Ms. Frasco.

"So we're certain this Felicity Frasco was really Wanda?"

"The manager of the hotel identified the photograph instantly, according to the report," Doris said. "Anyway, they were hardly discreet. Of course, we don't have photographs showing them having sex. But they were spooning all over the place, and carrying on in and around the pool in ways that some of the other guests found pretty offensive. And, for what it's worth, she was graphic in her language."

"Well, that's our Wanda."

"And this Mr. Frasco? I suppose that's not his name either."

"Don't know who he is. He wasn't what we were looking for. I suppose it was Dennis, but I wouldn't be surprised if Wanda had other men on her hook."

I was sorry we had no picture of Dennis. But it was too late for that. In any event, shortly after the hotel episode, Wanda booked a flight on Qantas to San Francisco under yet another name, and with what was apparently a forged Australian passport. She traveled alone. An Earl Frasco, whoever that was, did not go with her.

In San Francisco, she moved from motel to motel, and this time she had a companion, Dennis Little, who appeared from out of nowhere. The reports had very little to say about Dennis, but after all Wanda was the subject, not Dennis. In San Francisco, she lived modestly and avoided luxury hotels. But San Francisco is a very expensive city, and it was not at all clear what she was living on.

The investigators had, obviously, spent time snooping around the various places where Wanda and Dennis had taken up residence. Wanda was pregnant by this time. It was unclear whether she became pregnant in Australia, in the United States, or perhaps on the long Qantas flight from Sydney to San Francisco. The report did not commit itself on that question, but I think I knew the answer.

Wanda and Dennis lived quietly, rarely went out of their motel, and saw almost no one. There was one occasional visitor: an old man in his 80's. Nobody could identify this man, but my guess was that this was either Simon or Rupert Mobius. Since Rupert died early in the year, I suppose it was Simon Mobius. By late summer, she was clearly pregnant, and the visits were a startling, and (I thought) rather significant, fact.

Derek said: "I don't know about our grandfather. But she definitely saw Uncle Rupert."

I asked him: "What makes you think so?"

"Well, when I met Wanda, I felt she seemed vaguely familiar. I knew I saw her somewhere before, but I couldn't put my finger on where. But now I know."

"OK, tell me."

"I was going to have dinner with a friend of mine, guy who works for Google, I don't know what he does, something technical; we've been friends for years, since high school actually. And we were going to meet in the city at an Italian restaurant, doesn't matter which one. I parked my car in a parking ramp. This was sometime in February, I think. I was walking a couple of blocks, and I passed by this fast-food joint, and I was surprised to see my uncle Rupert, he was sitting at a table looking like a bum, but of course that's the way he always looked. He was having a heart-to-heart talk with a young woman, and I thought to myself, the old devil! For a minute I thought about going inside and saying hello and finding out, who's the chick; but I was in a hurry, and I was late, so I just kept on going."

"And that was Wanda?"

"Well, I didn't know who it was, she was a total stranger, but yes, now I realize, it was Wanda. I mean, I can't be 100% sure, and if you put me on the stand, in a courtroom, I'd have to say, I *think* it was Wanda Skadden, but as to taking an oath, no way. Still, Frank, I don't want to sound like I'm contradicting myself, but it *was* Wanda Skadden."

"And what do you make of that?"

"I honestly don't know. But maybe she told him she was pregnant or was going to be, soon, and that the father of the child would be his nephew Piers."

"Why do you think so?"

"Well, for one thing," Derek said, "it explains something that was pretty funny. My grandfather, in his 'confession,' or whatever you want to call it, said something about grandchildren present and future, and I thought, this must be a mistake, he's got the only two grandchildren he's ever going to have, he must have meant great-grandchildren. But now I think Grampa knew about Wanda... that he found out, at some point, that she was pregnant."

"Maybe Rupert told him she was pregnant, or was planning to get pregnant?"

"It figures, no? Uncle Rupert knew Wanda was planning on getting pregnant, and he told Grampa, hey, look bro, you're going to become a grandpa again. Or Wanda told him later. That's possible too."

My brain was whirling. This seemed a likely scenario. But what did that mean about the strange death of Rupert Mobius? The first thing that popped into my head was the idea that it made Wanda the number one suspect. After all, why did she come to the States in the first place? True, she had to get out of Australia; she faced arrest there. Did she come here to collect money for an unborn baby? But she wasn't pregnant yet....

I know she gave us a graphic description of how she impregnated herself. But the woman was a pathological liar. Anyway, she told her plans to Rupert—she must have known he was rich: people like Wanda have a kind of radar, they can smell a rich man from miles off, the way a vulture sniffs a rotting carcass. She was probably trying to get some money out of him. Maybe she told Simon, but she didn't need to. Rupert would do that.

Interesting: Simon never breathed a word of this— assuming he knew—to his own grandchildren. Why?

We know from Gideon that there was talk about changing the will. Did that stimulate Wanda to make her move? Get rid of the old man, as a kind of guarantee for her baby, soon to be born?

For that matter, didn't it give Simon an additional motive for killing his brother?

But was Wanda anywhere near the apartment the day Rupert died? There was nothing to suggest that she was. Still, it was easy to go in and out of the building without anybody seeing you. Wouldn't Fern have seen her, though?

One other thing about the reports: something that struck me as extremely odd and out of character. Wanda went to church. That would have been startling enough. The particular church was even more interesting. It was a fringe church, called the Church of Christian Possibility. The church was a small building in the Mission District; and it was presided over by the Reverend Elijah Foster-Morrison. This could hardly be a coincidence. I had the feeling Wanda went to church for reasons other than spiritual comfort.

I felt I had to talk to Wanda again. I have to admit, I felt a little guilty. It was somewhat irregular. Also, I did it on my own. I never checked with my clients. Or with my wife, who would have voiced extreme disapproval. But there were questions I simply had to ask Wanda Skadden.

She came with the baby, to my office. The baby was wrapped in a somewhat dirty pink blanket. Fortunately, he was fast asleep.

"Cute little thing," I said, smiling at Wanda, as she sat down.

She sneered at me. "Cute my ass. Babies are all the same. I could have gotten him on Craigslist, for all you know. Well, you know I didn't. DNA doesn't lie. I only wish... I mean, this kid, he's driving me nuts. It's 24/7, you know that? Do you have kids?"

"I do."

"Yeah, but your wife probably did all the work. You took out the garbage. I swear, I better get a lot of money out of this. Otherwise, I'd just as soon put the kid up for adoption."

You had to feel sorry for little Piers, Jr. He would surely be better off with Doris.

I changed the subject: "You were in the country when Rupert Mobius died."

"Yes, I was. So what? So were three hundred million other people. Are you insinuating something?"

"You saw Rupert Mobius. You had meetings with him. Why, Wanda?"

"What is this, the third degree? Why is it any of your business?"

Of course, it wasn't. I pressed on: "Did you tell him about your plans for the baby? And did you see Simon, too?"

"Simon? I'm not going to answer. But Rupert, yes. I told the old cheapskate about the baby. Is that a crime? I thought he'd be interested. Piers always told me his uncle had a soft spot for him. So I thought he might want to know. I got a kick out of telling him. He nearly dropped his false teeth."

"He was surprised, right?"

"Sure. Anyway, in case you didn't know, he was nutty as a fruitcake. And he had that other total nut, Plotnick— she was giddy with excitement about the idea of a baby. Oh my, she said, in her crazy voice, this is so exciting. Because this wasn't going to be Piers Mobius's baby, it was going to be Piers Mobius *himself*, coming back to life, like that Tibetan guy. Reincarnation. She really believed that. And I think Rupert Mobius half believed it himself."

I went right to the point: "Did he give you money? Did Rupert Mobius give you money?"

"I'm not going to answer that. I'll take the Fifth Amendment. Not that I really understand what that is. I'm Australian, and proud of it."

"It means, you don't have to answer questions in court, if they might incriminate you. That's basically what the Fifth Amendment says."

"Well, I'm not going to answer. I just don't want to. There's nothing incriminating, don't get me wrong. What Rupert Mobius did or didn't do with his own money, that was totally his business, no?"

I said: "OK. So he did give you money."

"So what? I was broke, and the baby would be part of his family. It's not like I was blackmailing him."

I wanted to ask Wanda about her dealings with the Reverend Elijah Foster-Morrison; but I suspected I would get nothing more out of her. I had learned enough. The mystery of the payments, Rupert's payments, had been solved—though I imagined she had to use all her con-woman skills to talk him out of that much money with such a bizarre story. The picture was getting clearer. Yes, I was coming to some definite conclusions about Wanda. And about the strange death of Rupert Mobius.

30

A few days later, Doris received a supplementary report from her investigators.

It was fascinating reading. Turns out, Wanda was even more of a scoundrel than we thought. That she was a fake, a fraud, and a schemer: that much we knew. But we never thought she was capable of violence. Of murder, perhaps.

It seems the boat accident that cost Piers Mobius his life was extremely fishy. In fact, the local police, in Brisbane, were convinced it was no accident. They thought the boat was sabotaged. Apparently quite recently, they were actually able to salvage the wreckage, which was a few miles offshore. The report went into some technical details which I didn't understand, but the upshot was they were convinced someone had deliberately damaged the boat in some way.

But who? That wasn't at all clear, but the number one suspect was a woman named Anna Bock; at any rate, that's the name she was born with. We know her as Wanda Skadden. There were witnesses who had seen her in the general area the day before the accident, and on the very day of the accident her behavior was odd and suspicious. She was seen at the harbor, and there were indications she may have rented a boat herself. There was an ongoing investigation (I wondered exactly how "ongoing" it could be, after more than a year), and the police were very stingy with information. At any rate, they seemed to be proceeding on the theory that Anna Bock had somehow tampered with the boat. Exactly what her motive might have been was somewhat murky, but they did note that she and Mobius had been romantically involved. This had apparently come to an end, perhaps not a friendly end. In any event, our friend Wanda was suspected of murder. The murder of Piers Mobius!

This was indeed sensational news. Doris wondered whether "Wanda" might have had a hand in the death of Rupert Mobius as well.

"Mind you," Doris said, "this is just suspicion. She might be completely innocent, of *that*. But it just doesn't smell right."

Killing Piers Mobius, or for that matter Rupert Mobius, would of course land our Wanda in deep trouble. But neither murder—I can't help thinking in legal terms—would affect whatever rights her little boy had in the estates of his great-uncle and grandfather. It would, of course, be a great boon to Doris and her quest for custody of little Piers.

I was thinking, again, about old Simon's confession. If that confession was false, then the old man *was* trying to protect somebody. But who? My first guess had been Derek, and we know Derek was at the scene that fateful day. Now I'm wondering: did it have something to do with his future grandson? Maybe the idea of little Piers, a reincarnation, if not literally, then symbolically, really tickled the old man.

And in that case, was it Wanda he wanted to protect? Maybe, as the mother of the child, she deserved protection. By the time he came up with the confession, she was in full bloom. We know the old man thought he had very little time to live. He had nothing to lose by confessing to a crime that he didn't commit. And he would save the skin of the kid's wayward mother.

Did this make sense? Not really. But then, what did?

I did a little checking on my own. I looked at the website of the church which the good Reverend Elijah was running. The text was mostly psychobabble, but one small fact caught my eye. The Reverend had founded the church, and it now had branches in three states, and also in Brisbane, Australia. Indeed. I wonder if the Reverend ever visited his flock in Australia.

I had a sudden, wild idea. It came to me in a flash. What was the connection between the Reverend and Wanda Skadden? Could it be that the "Earl Frasco" who spent time in a hotel in Brisbane with Wanda Skadden, was really the Reverend Elijah Foster-Morrison? I downloaded a photo of the Reverend from the website, and asked Doris to email it to her investigators and see if they could make an identification.

Meanwhile, I also asked Doris for copies of the various reports so that I could study them at my leisure. She agreed. There were a lot of interesting things about them. The chronology, for example. Was Wanda the key to the mystery? These little chats with Rupert and Simon.... They just had to be significant. To tell you the truth, ideas were beginning to form in my head. Hunches, intuitions. They could be all wrong, of course. They often are.

31

That night, Celia and I had a quiet dinner at home. My daughters had gone to visit friends. They do this often. My girls are gregarious; they love people. "People" of course means people their age. Parents are decidedly *not* people. Parents have many roles: furniture, food-providers, erupting volcanoes, creatures from outer space; but real honest-to-goodness people, almost never.

We ate leftovers and chewed over events of the day. I brought Celia up-to-date on the various Mobius issues. She was mildly disapproving, as she often is. "Frank, dear," she said. "Just stick to the law part. Forget the mysterious death of Rupert Mobius. It doesn't concern you."

"Oh, but it does," I said.

She was silent for a while: possibly she thought there was no point trying to persuade me. But then she said, "Funny thing, but something about the name Mobius rang a bell with me. Anyway, I was talking today to Adam Finkel. You remember him, don't you?"

"Was he the brother-in-law of the people next door?"

"Of course not. That was Alex Fink. Adam Finkel teaches math at my school. He's the one I told you about, the one with terrible skin, you know, it's really disfiguring, poor thing, he's tried everything, gone to a hundred dermatologists, and there's nothing they can do. Anyway, he's very sweet, and he tells me his troubles. And I happened to mention this Mobius affair, and he laughed, and said, mathematicians know all about Mobius."

"They do?"

"Well, not about the family, you know, the ones you're involved with. There was a German mathematician, August Mobius, and he invented the Mobius strip, or discovered it, or something."

I had a vague memory that I had heard something like this before. "The Mobius strip. What is that?"

"Well, it's a surface that has only one side, which sounds impossible, but math is all about impossible things, like the square root of minus one. I asked him, how can there be such a thing as a one-sided surface, and apparently, in mathematics there can be. Anyway: a Mobius strip has only one side, and if you take a strip of paper, sort-of twist it, and then join the two ends, you have a Mobius strip, and I tried it, and it really does have only one side, in a way."

"Amazing," I said. Then we took a strip of paper and made our own Mobius strip. Of course, it doesn't really have one side, but in a way it does. I can't explain it.

"Adam is so sweet," Celia said. "It's too bad about his complexion. How will he ever find a woman? And the students take advantage of him. He's too good-natured."

But Adam Finkel failed to interest me. The Mobius strip on the other hand did. I looked it up on the web. I found a very learned article about the Mobius strip, full of extremely mysterious equations. It also mentioned something equally mysterious called a Klein bottle, which is three-dimensional, or maybe four-dimensional, which was totally baffling to me, even though there's a company (this is actually true) which manufactures glass Klein bottles, and you can buy them. What you get is a "single sided bottle with no boundary. Its inside is its outside. It contains itself." I have to admit I have no idea what this could possibly mean, although there were pictures of Klein bottles on the website. Oh yes, and a whole gaggle of very impressive equations. I have no idea why anybody would buy a Klein bottle, since it seemed to have no earthly function. Maybe the same people who buy chocolate covered ants or certain types of fruitcake, things nobody ever actually uses, maybe they also buy Klein bottles.

I was mildly depressed by looking at these websites. It reminded me how ungifted I am in math and science. The kids today take Advanced Placement Calculus, can you imagine? My own older daughter is doing that. When I went to high school, I found even trigonometry baffling. In the end, after college, I took refuge in the study of law, where nobody has to know calculus or other forms of modern wizardry, and which demands no particular skill or, for that matter, not that much in the way of brain power.

Yet the Mobius strip and the Klein bottle stuck in my mind. And believe it or not they turned out to be meaningful. And very soon, too.

32

Yes, this may surprise you: but I was on the way to discovering who killed Rupert Mobius. And this despite the fact that I am not, in fact, a detective, nor do I have the kind of skill that the people have in mystery stories, you know, like Sherlock Holmes or Miss Marple. They are ferociously clever, and they never make a mistake, and they always solve the mystery in the end. Of course, the authors cheat: the authors are in complete control, and they make sure Miss Marple is always right and that her reasoning is always totally correct.

I'm not like that at all. I mean, I don't have that skill, any more than I have skill in calculus or other mathematical subjects (including the Mobius strip). So how did I manage in this case? How could I solve a mystery that the authorities with their forensic labs and so on, utterly failed to solve? Simple: because I knew the people involved. I knew things they couldn't have known, because they were not in human contact with the colorful cast of characters that orbited around the case of Rupert Mobius.

You see, a lot of things came together. First of all, I got a report from Doris' people in Australia. This had to do with my hunch about the Reverend Elijah and the mysterious Earl Frasco. Hunches are sometimes right. Where would the great detectives be, without their hunches?

This hunch turned out to be totally wrong. Nobody recognized the Reverend Elijah in Brisbane; and the investigator in this country discovered that, at the crucial times, the Reverend was in fact in Hot Springs, Arkansas, where he had rendezvoused with a female parishioner—a married one, at that. I was, however, totally uninterested in the sex life of the Reverend. If he wasn't Earl Frasco, I had no concern with him.

It was helpful, though, to cross this hunch off my list. And that led to even further thought. Something rang a bell. In fact, a number of bells. The first bell had to do with chronology. I had been aware for some time that Wanda had told me and others a huge pack of lies. All that stuff about the hotel in Brisbane: that she got pregnant there, and then celebrated or whatever, and then flew first class to the United States. None of that could possibly be true. Unless, of course, she was carrying the baby for ten or eleven months, maybe more. No, she was already in the United States when she got pregnant.

Crude and foolish lies. But Wanda was a reckless person. We knew that already. A risk-taker.

And the second thing: I thought long and hard about the photo album: why would the killer steal a photo album? I rejected of course the nonsense Fern Plotnick told us. The photo album was, apparently, nothing special. It had the usual contents: family pictures, for the most part. At least that's what Cranshaw said as he bemoaned the loss of pictures of his dear dead mother. Who else would be in the album? Simon, maybe. But why would anybody want to suppress pictures of Simon? Katerina and Cranshaw? No reason. Who else?

Who else, then?

One obvious person: someone who might not want any photographs around, someone who did not want to be recognized. That's when the wheels and the gears in my brain really started moving. I read over the reports, again and again. And I thought about Wanda's pregnancy. Almost certainly, as I said, she was in the States *before* she got pregnant. The rest was a fairy tale.

I had no window into Wanda's bedroom, but everything suggested that other parts of her story were lies. All that nonsense about abstaining from sex with Dennis. She said she wanted to be sure that it was the child of Piers Mobius. And that meant....

That's when it came to me in a blinding flash. I knew the scoundrel who killed Rupert Mobius. Of course Wanda was herself a scoundrel, and the Reverend no doubt was also a scoundrel. But the true scoundrel, the scoundrel of scoundrels, the man capable of anything, the man who was truly unscrupulous, capable of anything, including murder, was Piers Mobius himself.

Piers Mobius was alive and well. And Piers Mobius had been the other person in Rupert's apartment on that fateful day. He had been there and killed his uncle in cold blood.

33

But, you say, Piers Mobius was dead. He died in a boating accident. Had he come back to life? Was Fern Plotnick right?

In fact, he was never dead. It was all a trick. Australia was getting a bit too hot for him, and for Wanda too, for that matter. Nobody, however, would try to put a dead man in jail. Piers, in short, was the man we knew as Dennis Little. He was also Earl Frasco, and who knows what other names he went by. But his name, at birth, was Piers Mobius. A living, breathing Mobius, frisky enough to father a child with his girlfriend, his partner in crime, Wanda Skadden, or Anna Bock or any of her other names.

Little things popped back into my mind. Piers Mobius bugged out when his children were born: did he do the same thing with little Piers Mobius, Jr.? Maybe. More than likely, though, Wanda wanted him to go—to leave a place where somebody just might possibly recognize him and put two and two together. No doubt they had plans to meet again as soon as she could get her hands on some of the money.

They were as bold as brass, the two of them. Too bold at times. I remember how Dennis—or Piers—had tried to shut Wanda up when she was talking too much and behaving indiscreetly. But he himself had colossal gall. He was nervy enough to run up a huge hotel bill and then decamp in the middle of the night with his girlfriend. And nervy enough to call himself "Little," which in German is

"Klein," and "Frasco," which is the Italian word for bottle. Klein bottle: his little joke. Mobius strips and Klein bottles.

Now, suddenly, everything made sense. No, Wanda had not sabotaged the boat Piers Mobius was on. Or if she had, it was after making sure he could escape to wherever she had arranged for him. Probably to the boat she had rented. And then, to assume a new identity. And then to travel to America, but not on the same plane as Wanda. He had, I suppose, a forged passport. He and Wanda were used to changing names and identities anyway. Back home, he ran little risk of being recognized by anybody except his ex-wife, but he was most unlikely to see her. And, of course, he would be recognized by Simon and Rupert Mobius. But they would be sure to keep his secret.

What he and Wanda wanted was money. He could hardly try to claim any money as Piers Mobius: he was supposed to be dead. I think there was some attempt to befuddle Rupert, appearing now and then as if a spirit from the world of the dead—but the main thrust was to get his hands on some of the inheritance. Wanda's pregnancy was a gift from heaven. Whether it was really planned in advance or was simply an accident is something we might never know. Under normal circumstances, Wanda would make sure she would never be a mother: she was not the type. But the kid was a potential gold mine, and this changed her attitude. And Piers's.

Did he kill Rupert in cold blood? Was it planned? Or was it something on the spur of the moment? It hardly mattered. What I suspect is that Rupert, old and muddled as he was, began to realize what was going on: he had been paying money to Wanda, to help her carry the child of Piers. Maybe he became suspicious of her, or maybe he too thought she was a fraud. He planned to change his will. Whatever the situation, Piers decided it was necessary to act, and act quickly. Simon Mobius may have arrived on the scene at an awkward time. Either that, or his son called him and told him what had happened.

What kind of excuse he gave the old man, I have no idea.

Piers Mobius took the photo album for obvious reasons. He wanted no photographs of himself lying around. And after the baby was born, he quickly disappeared. Wanda of course knew where he was. It was important for him to lie low. Not that he ran much risk. Who would suspect a dead man? For that matter, who would suspect the shadowy boyfriend, Dennis Little, who had no obvious motive? He and Wanda could get together in some other country, Canada maybe... or in Europe, with the money.

Simon Mobius "confessed" to the crime. I had always thought he must be protecting somebody. And indeed he was. He was trying to protect his only son, his long-lost son. Had he been in some sort of contact with Piers all these years? I have a suspicion that he was, but we'll never know.

It all made perfect sense. Of course, I had no real evidence to back any of it up. Would anybody listen to me, if I broadcast this weird tale about a man pretending to be dead, about a Klein bottle, a photo album, and all the rest of it. And then I had to think of my clients, Derek and Doris. I could hardly imagine calling them and saying: Oh, by the way, I have good news and bad news. The good news is your father isn't dead. The bad news is, he's a fugitive from justice; and he's the one who killed your great-uncle Rupert.

But I did make use of one of my rare contacts with the criminal justice system. I spoke to Nolan Thom, a friend of mine and an ace criminal lawyer. I told him the whole story. I wanted him to talk to the authorities, the police, or whoever was relevant. Nolan works on the defendant side. In his line of work, he defends people like Piers Mobius and Wanda Skadden. But he curbed his defense-minded impulse, and got the tale to the police. There was a lot of back-and-forth across the Pacific, and I gather that somehow the story clicked; and it was shown that "Earl Frasco" was indeed Piers Mobius, who was extremely undead.

Police on two continents launched a search for Piers Mobius. As far as I know, they never found him. I am reasonably sure he isn't in the United States, or Australia for that matter; he's somewhere else, living no doubt under some other name. He never got any of the money, of course; but he is used to living by his wits. Perhaps the police will catch up to him someday. I wonder.

34

That was the end of the murder part of the story. I never told Derek and Doris about my role in solving the case. I let them think it was pure police work. I let them find out from other sources, not from me, about Piers Mobius and his misdeeds. Naturally, they found the news disturbing. Who wants to hear that your father is a killer? But they had never known him, and they were able to get over their dismay rather quickly.

Of course, the two estates were still a problem. Still hopelessly entangled and still enveloped in litigation.

Piers, of course, had no right to inherit from his uncle, or from his father: that was beyond question. Rupert's will was still under attack. Indeed, Katerina and Cranshaw now had another string to their bow. Rupert was not only old, and sick: he was under all these "undue influences"—Fern Plotnick, the Reverend, and, most significantly, his evil nephew, who came to him as a "spirit," and totally befuddled the old man. That was their argument. Katerina insisted they were going to win.

They wanted, as you know, to break the will; failing that, to put an end to what they called the "crackpot foundation" before it even got started. Somehow, word had gotten out about the will—and the fact that there was real money behind it. All sorts of organizations tried to intervene in the case: they argued that the trust was valid but could not be carried out as written. Other organizations, like the National Association for Psychic Research, were willing to take over. Gideon had his hands full trying to fight them off. They invoked the doctrine of *cy pres*, which you don't want to know about, but which gave them a reasonable shot at success.

Yet there was at long last a kind of happy ending. Gideon managed to work out a grand settlement to which everybody finally agreed, and which the Probate Judge approved. Gideon had a good deal of help from me, if I do say so. Even though I don't have a fancy office in San Francisco; even though I don't own a handmade Armenian rug.

The settlement agreement called for secrecy. We were none of us supposed to reveal the precise details. But I can share with you its general outlines. Somehow, Fern Plotnick was persuaded to resign as trustee, and the Reverend Milton Schwartz, aka Elijah Foster-Morrison, also tendered his resignation. The family agreed to pay them a substantial sum of money. They were not crazy enough to refuse. The Reverend could use the money to defend himself against two lawsuits claiming fraud, and three accusing him of sexual harassment.

The foundation was dissolved, but a large payment was made to a Center for Extrasensory Studies located at the University of Eastern Nebraska, which will (to an extent) carry on the work, though surely not the way Rupert Mobius wanted.

All this cost a lot of money. But the estate was huge. Katerina and Cranshaw ended up with several million each. My own clients, Doris and Derek, got less than they had hoped for, but it was still a substantial amount of money.

And what became of poor little Piers Mobius, Jr.? He too was awarded a share of the money. In a way, his mother's dream came true. He was going to be a rich little boy. Alas, it would do Wanda no good. She faced charges as some sort of accomplice in the murder of Rupert Mobius; on top of that, there were fraud charges in Australia. Doris went to family court to win custody of her baby brother. The parents were both fugitives from justice, she claimed (correctly), and the mother, moreover, had very little interest in her child.

Wanda gave up. First of all, she had no vocation for motherhood. Years of changing diapers, wiping the kid's nose and bottom, feeding him and nurturing him: this was not part of her plan. The money was no longer worth it. The image of prison loomed large. She too is now among the missing. I suppose she may be somewhere in this big wide world, along with her boyfriend perhaps. They are almost surely up to no good.

The little child did not know it, but lady luck was smiling on him, despite his unconventional conception and birth. Doris truly loved the baby. She is sure to be a devoted mother-substitute. So here there is something of a happy ending.

Eventually, the estates of Rupert and Simon Mobius ran their course, the assets were distributed to heirs and beneficiaries; the files were closed, and this saga came to an end. Oh yes, the lawyers. That's mainly Gideon and me. Gideon got a substantial fee: the statutory fees and on top of those, "extraordinary fees," with the approval of the Probate Court. He earned the money. It was a bittersweet victory for him. Ms. Guthrie quit her job, and as a parting shot told Gideon's wife about their affair: that brought his marriage to an end. Mrs. Grambling got a hefty settlement, which ate up his fees and a good chunk of his savings and his property. She got the condo at Lake Tahoe and the house in Woodside. It will take him years to make up for these losses. I hope Ms. Guthrie is satisfied.

I, on the other hand, have a healthy, stable marriage. There is no Ms. Guthrie lurking in the background. I too got substantial fees. We are thinking of a trip to Paris, Celia and I. We deserve it. I'll keep my eyes open, while there, for Piers Mobius and Wanda Skadden.

About the author

Lawrence Friedman is a professor of law at Stanford University. He teaches courses in American legal history and law and society. He is the author of *A History of American Law*, *Crime and Punishment in American History*, *The Human Rights Culture*, and *Total Justice*, among other works. He recently published *Dead Hands: A Social History of Wills, Trusts, and Inheritances*, a subject which is the backbone of Frank May's (fictional) practice.

Visit us at *www.qpbooks.com*.